Paupers, Parties
and Plagues

Wisdom
Editions

Minneapolis

Second Edition July 2023
Paupers, Parties and Plagues:
The Story of Everyday German Peasants Vol. 2, 1450-1850
Copyright © 2023 by David Koehler
All rights reserved.

10 9 8 7 6 5 4 3 2 1

ISBN: 978-1-960250-90-2

Cover and book design by Gary Lindberg

Paupers, Parties and Plagues

The History of Everyday German Peasants
Vol. 2, 1450–1850 AD

David Koehler

Wisdom
Editions
Minneapolis

Contents

Introduction

I have been interested in learning more about my German ancestors for some time. With the help of some very kind German researchers, I have been able to identify the names as well as the birth and death dates of some of my ancestors going back to the Thirty Years' War. But these bare facts have only increased my curiosity to learn more. What did they eat and drink? What were their homes like? How did they earn a living? How did they survive the wars, plagues and famines? What sort of medical care did they have? What was their standard of living?

I wanted to dig even deeper. What were the typical sights, smells and sounds that filled their days? What did they worry about? What was their self-image? What was their sense of time and place? These questions gnawed at me. I looked in vain for a single book that would answer my questions.

I found rich books about everyday life in the medieval period, but everyday life in the Iron Age was very sketchy. I was surprised to find it quite difficult to get good answers about everyday life after the medieval period. Both the early modern period and the recent period dealt with almost everything other than the nitty-gritty of daily life and how it changed.

Since the book I was looking for did not seem to be available, I decided to research the subject and write the book myself and share it with my cousins. It was easy to establish a focus for my research. Since 80 to 90 percent of Germans prior to 1850 were peasants, I would simply research the everyday life of German peasants. Simple enough. But what time period should I cover? There seemed to be no satisfying answer to that, so I included the entire historical period going back to 100 BCE when the Romans began writing about the German people.

Now the book began to take shape. I would research the period from 100 BCE to about 1850 when my German ancestors joined the tide of migration to America. I organized the book into five time periods corresponding to definable eras in German history. For example, the first chapter would start in 100 BCE with the first observations of the Romans about their German neighbors to the north. That first chapter would end with the overthrow of the Roman Empire in about 476 CE. I picked out a couple dozen subjects that interested me. For example, "What did they eat and drink?" would be a focused subject in each of the time periods.

This would not be a book about wars and dates, kings and generals. That was the history of my early school years. The protagonists of this book would be the men, women and children who are usually anonymous— the countless, faceless peasants. It would be a book about the nitty-gritty of their everyday lives.

I must admit that when I first began my research, I paused with some questions about my ability and credentials to embark on this project. I am not a professional historian. I don't have access to the primary sources. I don't have the languages—German, but also French, Latin and Old English—to decipher those primary sources. I don't have a Ph.D. I have not been trained in the disciplines of professional historians. Nevertheless, the book I wanted to read did not seem to have been written. So, I decided to give it my best effort and publish it. My audience would be my German-American cousins, some historical societies, and anyone else who might be interested.

I decided to try to offset my lack of professional qualifications with plenty of "perspiration." Over the past seven years, I have listened to a number of lectures on tape and read dozens of books. I decided to buttress my writing with a battery of endnotes. I also decided to encourage revisions and corrections by readers who might want to provide comments.

I invite and encourage comments, revisions, possible corrections. Write to me at davidjonkoehler@gmail.com.

David Koehler
August 2019

Part One:
1450–1650
The Early Modern Period

The bookends of 1450 to 1650

The years initiated by the Renaissance in Europe are often labeled the "Early Modern Period." This is the period from 1500 to 1800. I am using a slightly different time frame. I have chosen to begin this chapter immediately following Gutenberg's invention of movable type in 1450. That date seemed like a key milestone in inaugurating the early modern period. That gave me a starting point for this chapter.

I wanted to use two chapters to cover the approximate four-hundred-year period spanning from 1450 to the years when my ancestors left Germany. My German ancestors migrated from Germany to America between 1854 and 1882. So, 1850 is an approximate ending date for this story. I have decided to end this chapter in 1650, right after the end of the Thirty Years' War. The final chapter will cover the years from 1650 to about 1850, which I label simply "the recent period."

So the bookends for this chapter are the invention of the movable type press and the end of the Thirty Years' War.

Major historical events

The three major historical events of the period from 1450 to 1650 were:

1. 1517: The beginning of the Reformation in Germany
2. 1524: The outbreak of the Peasant Revolt in Germany and "what if?"
3. 1618–1648: The Thirty Years' War

1517: The beginning of the Reformation in Germany

First, on October 31, 1517, a Roman Catholic monk of the Augustinian Order in Wittenberg, Germany, named Martin Luther, nailed a list of 95 theses on the door of the castle church in Wittenberg to invite a debate. That action triggered a firestorm. Luther was called to account for himself at a judicial hearing by the Roman Catholic authorities. He was then excommunicated. Luther persevered. He probed deeper into his beliefs, and when his criticisms of the Roman Catholic Church could not be answered to his satisfaction, he became more outspoken.

A number of rulers in the German lands resented the Papacy in Rome and objected to the money-raising strategies that funneled money out of the pockets of German people into the coffers of the pope to rebuild the Cathedral of St. Peter and other papal projects. The local Saxon prince provided sanctuary for Luther in a castle where he translated the New Testament into the vernacular German spoken in the marketplace. Suddenly the Holy Scriptures were accessible to many German churchgoers.

Once Luther attracted a following, the church split. Large segments of the Roman Catholic Church agreed with Martin Luther that the Roman Church was corrupt. They agreed that the money paid to Rome for indulgences to forgive sins and pave the way to heaven was wrong. They also agreed that the sole authority for Christian doctrine was the Scriptures and that all that was required for salvation was faith in the mercy of God. And they affirmed that every individual should trust his or her own conscience.

The Roman Catholic Church would fight back by ostracizing Martin Luther and defending its principles. It was called the Counter-Reformation. What is important is that Martin Luther broke the monopoly of the Roman Catholic Church. His version of the Christian faith spread through Germany and into Scandinavia. Other versions of "Protestants" appeared in Switzerland and then in England, Scotland, France and the Netherlands.

Luther nailed his 95 theses to the church door.

For fifteen hundred years, the Roman Catholic Church had reigned supreme—virtually unchallenged. Martin Luther changed all that with his call for reforms. The power of the clergy was weakened. The fear of hell was dented. The conscience of the individual was empowered, and there was no going back.

The Peasant Revolt of 1524–1525

The peasant revolt that began in 1524 was the largest popular uprising in Europe prior to the French Revolution of 1789. It started when the Countess of Lupfen in the southern part of the Black Forest ordered the serfs to collect small shells which she wanted to use as thread spools for her sewing. Because this came after a series of difficult harvests, her frivolity and indulgence infuriated the local serfs. The serfs had been encouraged by Luther to obey their own conscience. They spontaneously gathered to express their resentment. It was reported that twelve hundred peasants gathered in the immediate area, and the movement quickly spread north to the Rhine River, south to Lake Constance and west into Bavaria and the Tyrol. The peasants organized themselves and began to discuss a whole range of grievances. The peasants elected leaders, and those leaders translated the grievances into a list of demands in "Twelve Articles." Soon twenty-five thousand copies of the "Twelve Articles" were printed and distributed all over Germany.

The peasants resented the tithe collectors.

What is interesting is that the peasants thought they were dealing from strength. Over the past twenty-five years, the lot of the peasants in the German lands had improved. They were able to increase their income and get better prices for their surplus crops. They felt empowered to assert their rights.

The "Twelve Articles" spelled out their demands for reform against the nobles who were their landlords and also against the church. Against the landlords, they demanded:

1. The abolition of serfdom.
2. The abolition of death tolls.
3. The restoration of fishing and hunting rights in what had been the common lands.
4. The restoration of forest pastures to graze their own livestock.
5. A restriction on excessive labor requirements, taxes and rents.
6. An end to arbitrary justice.

Their emphasis was on "fairness" and a restoration of their former rights.

Against the church, they demanded an accounting of the "great tithe," in which they paid 10 percent of their crops to the church. (This 10 percent was based on their gross harvest, which included about 25 percent that they had to store for next year's seed, so it amounted to almost 15 percent of their consumable harvest.) They demanded that this 10 percent tithe be spent on public purposes aside from a reasonable amount set aside for the pastor's salary. Notice that they were not demanding a termination of the 10 percent tithe but rather a fair and transparent allocation of that money to the welfare of the community.

A peasant army gathered five thousand strong outside Ulm with their demands. The local lord began negotiations while at the same time moving his troops into advantageous positions. Then he broke off negotiations, and his army fired a volley into the peasant army, followed by an attack led by fifteen hundred mounted cavalry. The peasants retreated and were soon slaughtered.[1] This became the model for the ensuing battles of the war. The peasants were large in number, but they were almost all foot soldiers, and they found it difficult to defend themselves against cavalry charges. They were undisciplined, disorganized and poorly led. The peasants were also citizen-soldiers who returned periodically to work their farms.

The peasant foot soldiers were no match for the cavalry.

In total, their numbers dwarfed the numbers of the church and nobility, with as many as six hundred thousand peasant soldiers against less than ten thousand troops of the nobility and church who were defending the status quo. But the nobility and church were well-armed, and they were disciplined soldiers led by excellent military leaders.

Early in the war, the peasants captured a monastery and overwhelmed the castle at Weinsberg on Easter Sunday, April 16, 1525. In their fury, the peasants took out revenge and slaughtered the defenders. It was called the Weinsberg Massacre, and this key event turned Luther against the peasant cause. He wrote his pamphlet *Against the Murderous, Thieving Hordes of Peasants*, in which he urged the princes to cut down the peasants like mad dogs.

The peasants lost battle after battle. Their leaders were executed and often burned at the stake. While the army of the nobility and church suffered few casualties, the peasants suffered enormous losses—up to one hundred thousand of the six hundred thousand peasant combatants were killed. Before the end of 1525, it was all over. The peasant revolt died in a whimper.

In the aftermath, the church leaders and nobility engaged in a renewal of repression. They were both afraid and angry after the revolt, and they wanted to punish the rebellious peasants. Furthermore, their military victory emboldened them to adopt policies of absolute rule. The end result is that the living conditions of the peasants worsened significantly after 1525.

What if?

I want to pause for a moment and reflect on "What if?" Britain's most popular historian of the twentieth century, A. J. P. Taylor, wrote a widely influential book about Germany during the last days of World War II. It was entitled *The Course of German History*. It was written to serve as a guidebook to the allied leaders who would be responsible for occupying Germany after it was defeated. The author's purpose in writing the book was to explain the behavior of the German people, who had been aggressors in two world wars in the previous forty years. Many thoughtful people were asking, "What is wrong with the German people? Why are they so belligerent and warlike?"

His book was extremely critical of the German people. He argued that for hundreds of years, they seemed to lack common sense. The Germans didn't follow a middle road of moderation in political affairs, but rather they lurched from one extreme to the other. They seemed to resist reasonable leadership, but they were very vulnerable to a dogmatic strongman. When presented with a strongman, they became craven and submissive.

Taylor argued that this unusual behavior was explained by the history of Germany. The German lands did not have a history of the give and take of political compromise. The German people did not have a successful track record of participatory democracy. They lacked a blueprint for working collaboratively with other nations. According to Taylor, the general mentality of the Germans lagged behind the English and the French in their sense of personal empowerment.

Taylor carefully traced the history of Germany and showed that at key turning points (such as the revolution of 1848), the German people did not step forward and assert their rights. They failed to use a combination of diplomacy and force (if necessary) to insist on these rights. Taylor starts his critique of the German people with their failure to act decisively with the 1524 Peasant Revolt, and he levels his most serious criticism at Martin Luther.[2]

So, I ask, what if Luther had used his influence to support and guide the peasant revolt by appealing to the "better angels" of the princes and the peasants alike? What if he inserted himself into the original drafting of the "Twelve Articles" of 1524 so that they would appeal to a large consensus of reasonable peasant leaders as well as to the reason of the German princes? What if Luther used his personal prestige to influence his own prince, Frederick III of Saxony, to support major social reforms? What if Luther had influenced the peasant leaders to limit themselves to widely popular, reasonable reforms and thus gain wide support among peasants all over Germany? What if Luther had sought out military leaders who could devise military tactics for the peasants to defend themselves against the cavalry attacks? The Swiss peasants had used long pikes to defeat the cavalry of the nobility in one battle after another from 1315 to 1477. What if the defenders of the status quo found themselves on the losing side of each battle when they faced a much larger force of peasants who were ably led, armed with pikes and fought with discipline? I realize these are many "ifs," and we are appealing to "better angels." But what if?

In this scenario, the German lands would not be split evenly between Roman Catholic and Protestant. Instead, they would be overwhelmingly Protestant. Perhaps the German lands would enter into a period in which the rule of law would slowly replace the arbitrary force of the landlord. The German lands would now be united by religion as well as language, and they probably would move to become a united country much earlier than 1871. What if?

The Thirty Years' War: 1618 to 1648

The Peace of Augsburg, signed in 1555 by the Holy Roman Emperor, had established the rules for determining post-Reformation Catholic and Lutheran territories. Essentially it decreed that the territory would be either Catholic or Lutheran based on the religious affiliation of the ruling prince of that kingdom. The subjects in the respective territories were required to follow the religious affiliation of their prince or else they were required to emigrate to another territory. This worked reasonably well until princes began to convert to Calvinism—in Switzerland, Netherlands, Prussia and elsewhere.

Now each group—Catholics, Lutherans and Calvinists—felt on the defensive, and in 1608 a cluster of Lutheran rulers formed the Evangelical Union, and the Catholics responded the next year in forming the Catholic League.

Tensions rose and came to a head in 1619 when a staunch Catholic, Archduke Ferdinand II of Austria, was named the heir apparent to the throne of Bohemia (present-day Czech Republic), which was then mostly Lutheran. When Ferdinand sent his representatives to Prague to prepare for his rule, a group of Protestants rebelled and threw them out a window of the Prague Castle. It is now famously referred to as the "defenestration" ("out the window"). They landed on a dung heap and somehow survived their sixty-nine-foot fall, but this event infuriated Ferdinand, who called upon an Imperial army to take control of Prague.

The Catholic representatives were thrown out the window in Prague.

This caused the Evangelical Union to gather troops, and soon there were outbreaks of violence in the German lands. The battles continued for thirty years. What started out as a religious war soon evolved into a political battle for European power. Roman Catholic France had joined the Protestant cause when they became alarmed that the rival Catholic Habsburg Empire was beginning to surround them. Later, King Gustavus

Adolphus of Sweden intervened when it appeared that the buffer of Protestant areas in northern Germany was being threatened. He wanted to ensure that Sweden and its Lutheran allegiance were not attacked.

The fighting took place off and on for thirty years, almost completely on German lands. The mercenary armies on both sides usually lived off the land, which meant they looted local farms. It was a period when man's inhumanity to man reached a new low. It is estimated that the Swedish armies destroyed up to two thousand castles, eighteen hundred villages and fifteen hundred towns (a third of all German towns). The casualties were horrific, and they were mostly civilian. It is estimated that eight million died during these years—mostly civilians, from injuries, disease and famine. In some regions, 50 percent of the population died.

The war finally ended with the Peace of Westphalia in 1648, which mostly recognized the status quo of the religious affiliations prior to 1618.

New developments that gradually changed everyday lives

I have tried to differentiate "new developments that gradually changed everyday lives" from the category of "major historical events" of the same period. At times the lines are blurred. The new developments are movements rather than events. The new developments evolved gradually, whereas the major events took place on a specific date. The new developments were often difficult to trace to a cause or a beginning. New developments have had long-lasting results, sometimes extending into our present day.

For the period of 1450 to 1650, I have selected six "new developments." I included in this list the Reformation which I also listed under the major historical events.

> 1450–1600: Age of Exploration
> 1450: Books proliferate
> 1517: Reformation
> 1517: Rise of capitalism
> 1540: Coal begins to replace wood and charcoal
> 1550–1700: Scientific Revolution

1450–1600: Age of Exploration

Let us consider the Age of Exploration, which had an economic impact on the lives of our German peasants. The first seeds were planted in 1415, with Portugal sailing south and seizing the coastal city of Ceuta in North Africa, located directly across from Gibraltar. This encouraged the Portuguese to sail progressively farther south along the coast of West Africa. Eventually, Vasco da Gama rounded the Cape of Good Hope, and in 1498, he landed in the coastal city of Calicut in India. The Portuguese immediately established a profitable trade in spices beginning with pepper and cinnamon.

In 1492, Christopher Columbus, sailing for Spain, reached the "New World." This had momentous consequences with Spain quickly conquering Mexico and then Peru and sending back to Spain immense quantities of gold and silver as well as new food products—chocolate, corn, peppers and potatoes.

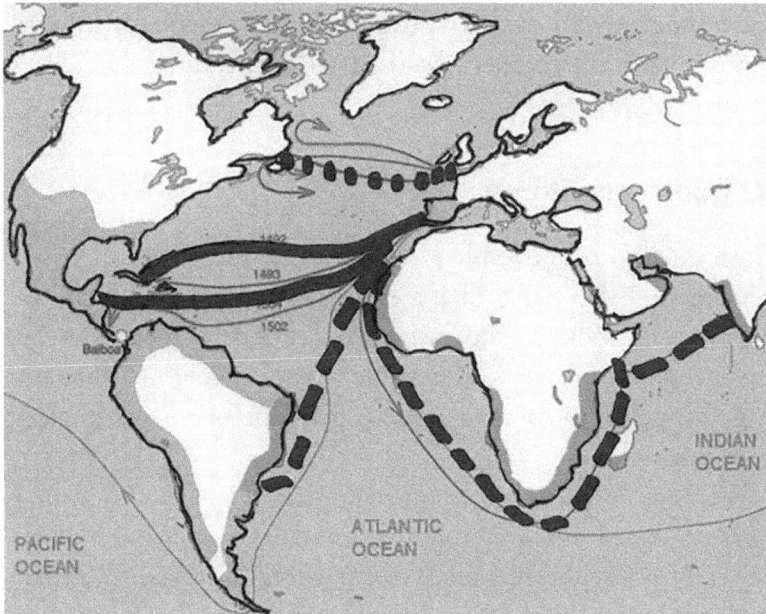

Between 1450 and 1600, the Portuguese reached Africa, India and Brazil. The English discovered the fishing waters off Nova Scotia, and the Spanish reached Central and South America. Because the Germans didn't have any seaports on the Atlantic, they fell behind during the Age of Exploration.

In 1494, Portugal claimed Brazil and began importing sugar to Europe. In 1497, John Cabot explored the north coast of North America and discovered its rich fisheries. This spawned the cod industry and became a valuable and popular food in Europe. A German mapmaker born in Freiburg named Martin Waldseemüeller created a new map of the world in 1507 that included the New World for the first time.

In 1511, the Portuguese seized Malacca in present-day Malaysia and established a base for its trading empire in rare spices. In 1522, the Magellan expedition returned to Europe after its three-year sail around the globe. In 1600 and 1602, the English and Dutch founded their respective East India trading companies.

All of these exploring companies were based in Atlantic seaports. Their gains in trade were made at the expense of Germany, which had no seaports on the Atlantic. German cities like Nuremberg and Augsburg had thrived during the medieval period as land-based trading centers, and now these quickly declined. The economy of Germany suffered as it now found itself at a competitive disadvantage in the increasingly global economy.

1450 Books proliferate

The introduction of moveable type and the printing press by Johannes Gutenberg in 1450 was a major event that laid the foundation for a proliferation of books in the ensuing one hundred years. This blizzard of books would not have been possible without two other developments that just happened to come together at the same time—cheap paper and effective ink.

The ancient world wrote on papyrus, a plant common in Egypt that was processed into long rolls and served as a good writing material. In the early 300s, the literate Western world switched to parchment. Parchment is untanned leather, and the best parchment is vellum which is the untanned skin of a very young calf or goat. The skin was scraped to remove all hair and then stretched and cut into a rectangular shape. Parchment presented one disadvantage. It was expensive. To produce a single two-hundred-page book required the skins of twelve sheep.

Paper mills in the 1500s produced inexpensive paper.

But there was an alternative. Paper was used as early as 100 CE in China and, in the 800s, by Arab writers. Paper is manufactured from a "soup" composed of a pulp of bits of cloth and water. A screen is dipped into this pulp mixture. The screen is then squeezed into a "pancake" to make it thin and to remove excess water. Then it is left to dry. The manufacture of paper was carried on by the Moors in the 1100s during their occupation of Spain. The Christians of Spain learned the process from the Moors. Italy had plenty of rivers and water mills, and by the 1300s, the center for paper manufacturing was focused in northern Italy. The rivers near Fabriano, Italy, powered waterwheels that activated large wooden mallets as well as cutters and nails, which tore rags to shreds to produce pulp.[3] Papermaking was carried out near swift-moving rivers. The cost of paper dropped very quickly. As early as 1400, a sheet of paper (the size to produce eight octavo pages) cost one penny in England.

Effective ink also arrived just in time for the new printing press. A water-based ink had been the standard ink used by scribes for hundreds of years. Ink was produced from a variety of recipes. One recipe called for ion salts to be mixed with tannin from gall nuts and a thickener. When applied to paper, it appeared bluish-black and gradually faded to dull brown. It worked well with a quill and could be made in different colors.[4] But the iron characters of the new printing press required a new type of ink. The ink had to be oil-based to work on iron characters, and ideally, it would be indelible. A new ink was invented for this purpose by grinding boiled linseed oil with lampblack or powdered charcoal.[5] Gradually, this was improved by mixing soot with turpentine (from pine trees) and walnut oil.

The happy convergence of the new printing press, with the new ink and the recently developed cheap paper, worked together to create a boom in book publishing. One source reports that by 1500, there were 236 different towns with a printing press, and twenty million books had been published.[6] Books were still relatively expensive, and print shops usually had to borrow the capital to acquire the necessary equipment. The Frankfurt Book Fair first opened in 1454 and continues to thrive today.[7]

The proliferation of books had two more results. First, "the rapid rise of the printing industry brought into existence a constellation of related crafts whose practitioners included printers, typefounders, engravers, compositors, woodblock cutters, proofreaders, booksellers and even peddlers." Second, the subject matter of many books was the sharing of basic knowledge. "A barrage of how-to-do-it manuals appeared in the tens of thousands of copies. The most widely circulated of these printed how-to-do-it books was a group of craft manuals known collectively as the *Kunstbuchlien* ("skills booklets"), which appeared in various German towns in the early 1530s."[8]

1517 The Reformation

The Reformation was an earthquake that broke many existing structures and gave birth to many new green shoots. Obviously, the Reformation broke the monopolistic power of the Roman Catholic Church and empowered not only the new Lutheran Church but also a Reformed

Church and a whole series of independent sects that sprang from the Anabaptist movement. But this is simply the ecclesiastical or theological aspect of the Reformation.

The Reformation also changed attitudes about sex, family life and vocation. Monasteries were closed. Priests were encouraged to marry and raise children. By implication sex was liberated at least within the bounds of Christian marriage. Vocation was reinterpreted. The highest calling was no longer to be a monk—praying in seclusion from the world. Instead, each person would serve God through their own occupation—whether farming or carpentry or making shoes. Daily work was now deemed holy.

1517 Rise of capitalism

The rise of capitalism was propelled in 1517 by the impact of the Reformation. John Calvin, Martin Luther and other reformation leaders adopted a new view toward individualism, work, money and money lending—all of which contributed to the rise of capitalism.

Let's start with individualism. The Reformation fanned the spirit of individualism. Each individual had a direct relationship with God. This emerging sense of individualism encouraged them to step away from the guild structure of the Middle Ages, and it made some of them entrepreneurs "who produced and sold in unrestrained competition. This spirit was an attitude toward life, a fury of work in gainful employ. This phenomenon was peculiar to the Western world. In the East, men would work in order to attain a certain standard of living and then stop."[9]

For centuries Roman Catholic monks had mostly eschewed labor—with some important exceptions. They pursued a higher calling—worship and prayer. Over the years, the monasteries had become rich, and many monks became fat and indulgent. But when one's daily work was consecrated, the money earned through hard work now took on a new meaning. Money began to lose its taint. Money became a good thing—a well-deserved reward for good work. Money was also recognized for the good it could accomplish. It could be invested in useful projects like bridges, roads, hospitals and churches. It could also be loaned out at a reasonable rate of interest to allow borrowers to have access to money to achieve a particular goal (such as setting up a business).

Roland Bainton, former distinguished professor of church history at Yale Divinity School, wrote, "In his [Luther's] eyes the occupations of the farmer, the doctor, the school teacher, the minister, the magistrate, the house-mother, the maidservant and the manservant were all of them religious callings, vocations in which one was bound to render no lip service but to work diligently as serving not merely an earthly but also a heavenly master."[10]

"Those who could work should work, and those who could not, should be supported, but none should beg."[11] Finally, Luther gave his blessing to that key feature of capitalism—banking and using money to make money. He approved of lending money at interest with the stipulation that "the rate did not exceed 5 percent."[12]

Both John Calvin and Martin Luther encouraged hard work, not spending money frivolously, but rather saving and investing money (to be loaned at 5 percent interest). They planted early seeds of capitalism.

1540: Coal begins to replace wood and charcoal

A fifth new development was the movement of coal replacing both wood and charcoal as fuel—for heating homes and cooking but also for industrial purposes such as to create energy for kilns and then later for steam engines. It all started in England when the cost of firewood began to escalate. In her book entitled *Coal*, historian Barbara Freese reports that "During the 1500s, the English faced an energy crisis brought on by an exploding population and dwindling forests. To deal with their problem, England became the first country in the world to mine and burn coal on a large scale beginning around 1575."[13]

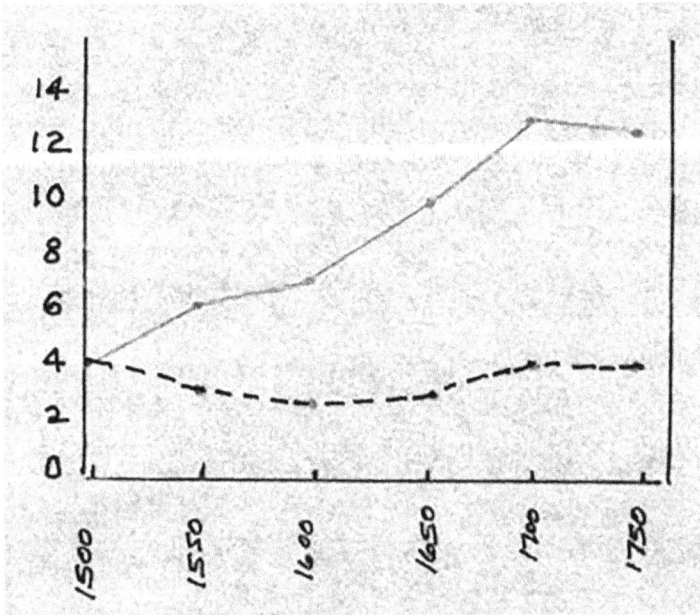

The graph above shows the divergence of prices of coal (the bottom line) and firewood (the top line) in the London market. The prices are expressed in terms of grams of silver it costs to generate a million BTUs of heat. As firewood became scarce between 1500 and 1750, its cost rose threefold while the cost of coal was unchanged. By 1750, England had converted to coal, which fueled its Industrial Revolution.

By the year of Queen Elizabeth's death in 1603, coal was the main source of fuel for England.[14] The historian Alan D. Dyer reports that the divergence began in about 1540 when the price of firewood began to rise. Soon charcoal also increased in price.[15] In the illustration, the top line reflects the sharp increase in the price of firewood, and the lower line reflects the price of coal, which remained virtually unchanged for several hundred years.

The German lands were more heavily wooded, but inevitably this same pattern moved to the German lands. Although the peasant masses were highly resistant to any kind of change, the reverberations were deeply felt.[16]

1550–1700: Scientific Revolution

The sixth new development was the Scientific Revolution which usually is dated from about 1550 to about 1700, and it is an important label for contemporary historians. It was triggered in 1543 by two different events. First, the Italian doctor Andreas Vesalius published his book *On the Fabric of the Human Body,* which became the foundation for modern biology. In that same year, Nicolaus Copernicus published *De Revolutionibus Orbium Coelestium (On the Revolutions of Celestial Bodies),* where he argued that the sun, not the earth, is the center of our solar system, and the earth and other planets revolve around the sun. Later Galileo reaffirmed this heliocentric solar system at his own peril.

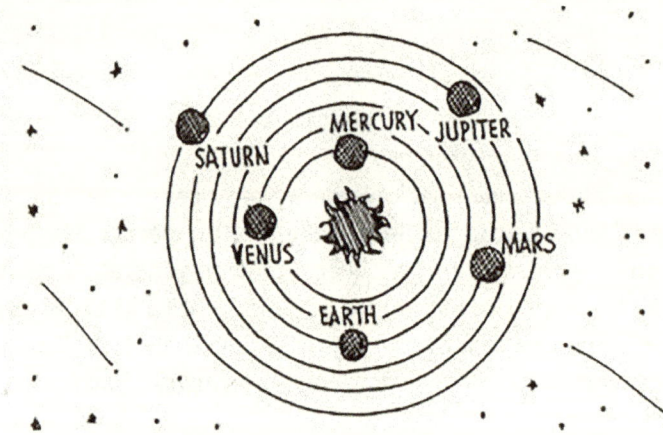

Finally, scientists proposed a heliocentric solar system.

Until recently, this one-hundred-fifty-year period was viewed as an unusual convergence of brilliant scientists making discoveries that changed the way educated people viewed their world. In 1591, Galileo Galilei demonstrated the laws of gravity. In 1618, Johannes Kepler explained why planets revolved in orbits in his Third and Final Law of Planetary Motion. In 1637, Rene Descartes wrote his *Geometry.* In 1643, Evangelista Torricelli invented the barometer. In 1656, Otto von Guericke invented the air pump and demonstrated the power of a vacuum when he arranged for two teams of sixteen horses to try (without success) to pull apart a tube held together by an air vacuum. Finally, in 1687, Isaac

Newton published his masterpiece *Principia Mathematica*. This book became the foundation for modern physics and astronomy.

Although none of these breakthroughs had immediate impacts on the daily lives of German peasants, they shaped new and rational ways for people to understand their world. Most importantly, this Scientific Revolution served as the foundation and precursor of the Enlightenment (sometimes called the "Age of Reason") which began in about 1700. The Enlightenment glorified *reason* and *the experimental method* as the way to truth as opposed to the previous thought patterns of superstition and acceptance of the teachings of ancient authorities.

The historian Clifford Conner makes a convincing case that the Scientific Revolution is misunderstood in two ways. First, he says, "Perhaps the process was too drawn out to be properly considered a revolution, but it utterly transformed the way we human beings understand the world around us." Second, he points out the "broader base" of the foundations of the Scientific Revolution. It was an era in which "simple workmen were capable of convicting of error all great men who are called philosophers."[17] In other words, illiterate German peasants learned from their own personal experience and observation. They ignored the "experts" whose conclusions flew in the face of their own hard experiences. Most of these people were illiterate, so they could not write down their conclusions and achievements. In fact, recently, historians have placed much more emphasis on the gradual empirical learning of common people accumulating know-how and insights to produce the Scientific Revolution.

It is ironic that this period of 1550 to 1700 corresponds exactly with the heyday of the witch trials and their obsession with superstition. From 1550 to 1700, an estimated seven thousand European women were executed for witchcraft.

How they lived

The changes in housing dating all the way back to 100 BCE have been modest and evolutionary, and this slow progress continued into the early modern age beginning in 1450. We will see some changes and improvements—more city dwellings, more multi-story houses, more glass used in windows, and more sturdy framing for houses that were built to last. These were all important upgrades in this period, but it is striking to note how many aspects of housing remained unchanged.

Furniture was primitive and scarce. For example, chairs lacked arms and backs. The lighting continued to depend upon candlelight or oil lamps, the heat continued to depend upon a fire in the fireplace, and there was no bathroom and no running water. Many houses remained one-room affairs. Many houses sheltered and protected domestic animals under the same roof. Most houses remained damp, dark and cold. Let's look at how they lived in the period of 1450 to 1650.

The Fachwerk style became dominant in the 1500s.

The most visible change was the new dominance of Fachwerk houses with their distinctive dark wooden beams and white plaster infill. These houses were built to last, and they have lasted to this day. If one visits the old town of any town in Germany, one sees these houses everywhere. This style dominated German house and barn building between 1450 and 1650.

The Albrecht Durer house was built in the 1400s in what was the new Fachwerk style. He lived in this house from 1508 to 1528.

By the 1600s, ceramic tiling was everywhere, even on the floors of modest homes. Until the 1500s, it was the custom to cover the floors of the ground floor rooms and the bedrooms with straw in winter and herbs and flowers in the summer. A doctor recommended rosemary, pennyroyal, oregano, marjoram, lavender, sage and other similar herbs.[18]

The French philosopher Michel de Montaigne traveled through the German lands in the late 1500s, and he noticed that there were several houses with glass windows.[19] Glass was a dramatic improvement. This was the first time that peasants enjoyed glass windows. Glass and oiled paper continued to be used simultaneously for quite some time. It is remarkable how slowly glass became standard for windows in Europe. Panes of glass were not commonly seen in Serbia until the 1800s. The windows continued to be closed using wooden shutters, which closed tightly from the outside.

We can imagine that the fireplace was a magnet in cold weather. Erasmus observed in 1527, "You go to the fireplace and there you take off your boots and put on your shoes, you change your shirt if you wish. You hang up your clothes, damp from the rain, near the fire and you draw near to the fire yourself."[20]

The habit of placing the bench in front of the fireplace probably gave rise to the narrow rectangular table; the guests sat on only one side of it with their backs to the fire and their stomachs to the table.[21] The cupboard became common in the 1500s. This was a vertical wooden piece with one or two doors protecting the articles within. The cupboard evolved into the cabinet, which featured drawers that slid in and out.

This man is relieving himself between two houses.

There had been no change in toilets. The "toilet" continued to be the traditional chamber pot, which was still emptied out the window. Prosperous peasants now enjoyed houses with multiple rooms, sometimes multiple bedrooms. Ideally, there was a chamber pot for each room. The illustration gives us evidence of second-floor latrines, and it shows that some simply relieved themselves in a convenient spot between two buildings.

At this time, there were cities in Germany (Nuremberg, Augsburg, Ulm) where there was not a sharp division between city and rural living. For instance, pigs enjoyed the freedom of the streets even in the largest cities.[22] The streets were so muddy that it was perilous to cross from one side to the other. The main streets of Frankfurt were hurriedly covered with straw or wood shavings on the eve of a fair such as the annual book fair. In the cities, the desirable land was precious, and therefore people built vertical houses of several stories. In these cities in 1500, sunlight rarely reached the ground. The second story of each building always jutted out over the first, the third over the second, and the fourth and fifth over those below so that at the top, neighbors could reach out and shake hands with those living across the street.

Typical sights, sounds and smells

This period brought some new sights, sounds and smells. The Thirty Years' War of 1618–1648 brought unwelcome sights such as clouds of dust that preceded an invading army coming to pillage, rape and murder. They often brought the sounds of foreign languages such as Swedish and French. Perhaps the most obvious new sound was the sound of explosions caused by gunpowder. There was the horrific loud noise of a cannon firing. A canon blast must have been deafening and terrifying. Gunfire from firearms—the predecessors of modern rifles—must have created a new sound—POP! POP!

Another sight was seeing naked people. These were destitute people who followed the customs from previous periods. When they were penniless and starving, they sold the clothes off their backs to buy a little food. Then they walked around naked until someone took mercy on them and gave them something to wear.

Another new sound was the noise of a water-powered sawmill. These became more common during this era. They were built in heavily wooded areas of the German lands so that the logs needed to be dragged only a short distance. The enabling technology was relatively new. A device was invented to convert the circular motion of a water wheel into the reciprocal, back and forth movement of a saw. So now sawmills were established in densely wooded areas along fast-moving streams. The sound was new—the squeaking of metal saw elements rubbing against each other, and the grating sound of the saw cutting through the log. This brought a pungent smell as well—fresh, moist sawdust.

Work

Let's start with the workload of the peasant wife. It had not changed in a thousand years. She was responsible for caring for her children, preparing the food, caring for the house, making and mending the family clothing, and helping to manufacture household items such as soap, candles and cooking utensils. When a family member was sick or injured, she was the nurse. She also tended the family garden plot, where she grew vegetables and herbs. She was responsible for the family's small farm animals—chickens, ducks and possibly sheep. She might also work in a "cottage industry" such as spinning thread from wool or flax. Finally, she helped her husband in the fields during critical times such as planting, haying in midsummer and harvesting the grain in the fall.[23]

Spinning thread or yarn was exclusively women's work.

By 1600, the peasant class had been differentiated into eight social classes that described the land ownership and work status of the man of the household. Here is a ranking in descending order:

1. Freisasse (or "Freibauer"): This was a peasant who owned a large farm and did not owe any duties to the landlord.
2. Vollmeier ("Vollspaenner" or "Hufner" or "Ackermann"): A peasant whose holding was a full holding which meant a large farm—usually sixty to one-hundred-and-twenty acres. He possessed a hereditary lease on that farm. He was prosperous and owned a full team of draft animals, such as four draft horses. He was obliged to use this team of horses for work on the landlord's farm or for transporting goods to market.
3. Halbmeier ("Halbspaenner" or "Halbbauer"): A peasant with a hereditary lease on a smaller farm—perhaps thirty to sixty acres and a smaller team, perhaps two draft horses. He was obligated to use that team in paying off his services to his landlord, whether in plowing or carting goods to market.
4. Hoefling: A person who held an office of some kind in the service of the landlord or the government.
5. Koether (or "Koetter"): This was sometimes translated as a "cottager," and this accurately described the person. This person owned a small cottage with a kitchen garden attached, and he may have had a very small landholding—not large enough to make a living. He may have had a little livestock but never a full team of draft animals. He had another main job—perhaps as a teacher or craftsman of some sort. He also hired himself out as a day laborer in busy seasons. These people had no share in the common pasture. This was a very common classification. In the German church records, I found that many of my ancestors were labeled "Koetter."
6. Brinksitzer: The brink was a hilly area near the village on land that was not considered arable. Those who lived here had little or no land, and they lived outside the protection of the village. They did odd jobs and were known to be available to run errands in the village.
7. Haeusling: This was a person living in a small house with no land. He may have owned the house, or he may have been a lodger.
8. Gesinde: This person was a live-in servant.

These rankings were very important to the peasants of the German lands.[24] They set apart the well-to-do peasants, and they marked those of inferior status. It functioned something like a caste system in which the higher-ranking people resisted seeing their children marry into a lower ranking.

As farmers have done forever, they gathered together and argued about the best grain crop to plant for the next year. Grain entered the human diet mostly in the form of porridge and bread. Rye and wheat made soggy porridges, but they made the best bread. Wheat was the most desired grain. It had a better texture than rye, tasted better, was more easily digested and its dough rose to a great volume. But wheat was a demanding grain in terms of soil and climate. It required good farming practices and regular fertilizing and grew best if it was not north of the 52nd parallel, so this ruled out growing wheat near Magdeburg, Hanover, Berlin, Hamburg, Bremen or Brandenburg.

Rye was the least demanding grain. It did not suffer from a lack of fertilizer, required less sunshine, had deep roots and endured freezing and thawing. Rye produced more straw (than wheat) and grew faster (thus making it easier to get rid of weeds).

Oats was a popular crop for animals. Horses thrived on it. But most humans didn't like oats, and they disparaged it as "animal food." Finally, there was barley. It could thrive in a wide variety of climates and had a short growing season, so it could be raised in cold climates. But it required regular tilling and weeding, and the yield was less than that of oats. Overall, rye was the easy favorite. Over the generations, most farmers opted for rye.

Horses preferred oats and thrived on a diet of oats. Many peasants used this as an excuse for their distaste for oats saying, "Oats are for animals."

Three hundred years later, in 1800, a survey in Germany revealed the following percentages:

> 41 percent of the land was planted in rye
> 25 percent in oats
> 19 percent in barley
> 8 percent in wheat
> 7 percent in spelt and buckwheat[25]

In the 1500s, one of the evolutionary changes was the continued migration to larger towns. The town became the hub for a growing workforce of skilled craftsmen. Most craftsmen belonged to a guild. The guilds were a hangover from medieval times. These guilds served the interests of the guild members (much like present-day labor unions). They established the standards of workmanship, fixed wages and prices. They made sure that apprentices received the proper training, and they carefully limited the number of people pursuing a craft in any one area. These guilds extended over many kinds of work—brewers, blacksmiths, printers, carpenters, masons, thatchers, shipwrights, weavers, miners, glassmakers, bridge engineers, minters and glove makers.[26]

Horses were always essential animals, and it seems that the horse was the first animal in which breeding became important. In the 1500s, Arab horses were much admired, and in England, Henry VIII had some Arab horses imported for breeding purposes. Louis XIV followed suit, and then Germany took an interest.[27] Horses grew in importance into the 1900s when the German states had 4.2 million horses.[28]

Horses created a whole industry devoted to their care. Every town was full of stables, and the shoeing smith was a person of substance. His establishment was rather like the present-day auto-repair garage where men would gather to talk and pass the time of day.[29] We read of a typical scene of this period: "There were long lines of carts overloaded with hay. They were awaiting purchasers—suppliers to the houses which kept horses and carriages. One buyer suddenly pulled out a fistful of hay, felt it, smelled it, and chewed it. He was on the staff of the Madame la Marquise."

In Augsburg in October during the 1500s, peasants offered piles of hay side by side with supplies of wood and game. In Nuremberg, peddlers with wheelbarrows sold the straw needed for the stables of the town. Horses steadily replaced oxen as draft animals. Horses provided travelers the means to move from one town to another. If the traveler needed to stay overnight, he got a room at a roadside inn. The inn was typically designed around a large stable with stalls for the horses in the middle and a row of rooms for lodgers along either side of the stable.

Hay was an important crop. Everyone in the family helped bring in the hay before the rain could spoil it.[30] Hay was used as feed for livestock during the winter.

Harvesting hay was a busy time for all.

Table talk: Starting a business to build Fachwerk houses in his hometown

Wolfgang Meyer is nineteen years old, and he is one of five apprentices for the master carpenter George Zimmerman. George Zimmerman is the only master carpenter in the city of Hanover and is the director of the local carpenter's guild. He is short and stocky with a grey beard and accustomed to giving orders. He has a stern demeanor but softened with kind blue eyes. He is in his fifties and lives in his large house, which serves as a home for his family and a boarding house for the five apprentices and several servants. The evening meal is over, and everyone else has departed. Wolfgang is tall and slender with a serious demeanor. It is a warm spring evening in the year 1649—just one year after the last fighting in the Thirty Years' War.

Wolfgang has waited until everyone else has left the dinner table, and now he begins, "Mr. Zimmerman, thank you for agreeing to meet with me privately. I have something quite serious to discuss with you."

Mr. Zimmerman: "Of course, Wolfgang. Go ahead."

Wolfgang: "I think I told you that two years ago, raiding soldiers killed my family. They stole everything they could carry with them, then they tied up my father and mother, my brother and my little sister inside the house, and they burned the house to the ground. My family is gone. They also burned the fields of the whole village of Abbensen. There is almost nothing left."

Mr. Zimmerman: "Yes, you told me after you came back from visiting the destruction. It's a terrible thing. But there is nothing we can do about that now."

Wolfgang: "Yes, of course. But I inherited the land, and my uncle has offered to buy the land from me. I am thinking of selling."

Mr. Zimmerman: "Well, that is certainly up to you. Do you think he is offering you a fair price?"

Wolfgang: "Oh, more than fair. But I am thinking of using the proceeds from selling the farm to set up my own business."

A carpenter at work in his workshop.

Now Mr. Zimmerman frowns. Wolfgang has two more years to serve his carpentry apprenticeship. He doesn't want Wolfgang to leave early and give up a chance to become a journeyman and member of the carpenters guild. But Mr. Zimmerman likes Wolfgang. He feels very sorry about Wolfgang losing his entire family, as well as the family home. He wants Wolfgang to make his way in the world. He decides to say nothing for the moment. He leans forward, nods his head, and says, "Tell me more."

Wolfgang: "I want to build Fachwerk houses back in my hometown of Abbensen. The Fachwerk houses are so much superior to the old one-story wattle and daub houses. They don't need to be rebuilt every generation. Some Fachwerk houses here in Hanover are already one hundred years old. The thing is, Abbensen still doesn't have a single Fachwerk house. It's a perfect opportunity."

Mr. Zimmerman agrees, "Well, they are built to last—perhaps hundreds of years. But there are two problems: First, these houses are not easy to construct. To begin with, you have to locate timbers and shape them into solid beams and pillars. Then you have to fashion joints and wooden pegs to attach these timbers securely to each other. Finally, you have to prepare a good infill to fill the spaces between the timbers. However, the second problem is that you won't be a member of the carpenter's guild until you finish your apprenticeship two years from now. No one is permitted to build houses unless they are members of the guild."

Now Wolfgang leans in toward Mr. Zimmerman. "Well, that's why I wanted to talk with you personally. You see, I have two cousins in Abbensen who have access to a forest of the perfect material for those timbers. I plan to hire those two in my own company. Thanks to you, I believe I have learned the skills necessary to make the joints and pegs and peg holes to fit the timbers together. And most important, I believe I have learned how to use concrete and pieces of stone and brick to make the finest infill. That is not what concerns me. What concerns me is the guild requirement. You see, there is no carpenter's guild in Abbensen. The village is too small. People usually build their own houses. The closest guild is here in Hanover."

Mr. Zimmerman leans back thoughtfully and asks, "How far is Abbensen from here?"

Wolfgang: "About fifteen miles."

Mr. Zimmerman: "I don't think you will have any trouble with the

Hanover carpenter's guild. If you are working in Abbensen, you won't be taking any jobs from us. I certainly won't get in your way. I might say that you are the best apprentice I have ever had. Since your parents died, I have thought of you as one of my family. I will miss you very much. You have my blessing to go into the house building business in Abbensen—guild or no guild. In fact, I have some extra tools to help you get started."

Wolfgang breathes a sigh of relief. He is going to put his skills to work. He will support himself. He will marry, have children and perpetuate the Meyer family line, and he will begin building houses that will last for hundreds of years.

What they ate and drank

In this time period, the eating and drinking habits of German peasants were as diverse as the peasants themselves. By this time, there were prosperous peasants and growing numbers of desperately poor peasants. Their eating habits were correspondingly different. For the poorest peasants, what they ate and drank remained the same as their ancestors from the late Middle Ages. It was bread accompanied by a one-pot porridge in the morning and by a one-pot soup for lunch and supper. Hence most of the cooking was carried out with one pot suspended over an open fire. This was little changed from a thousand years earlier.

A peasant family welcomes guests to their home. Notice the large kettle simmering over an open fire.

Their dinnerware remained wooden plates and bowls. They usually shared their dinnerware. Only people of the very highest rank had their own dishes, plates and drinking cups. Other people ate in pairs with one "cover," meaning a serving for two.[31] Each diner, however, had their own trencher, a thick slice of stale, unleavened bread measuring about six by four inches. In the 1400s, the bread trencher began to be superseded by a square of wood with a circular depression in the middle.

There were a few new foods and spices available, but only the prosperous peasants could afford them. For example, the poorest peasants stirred bread into watery vegetable stews.[32] Meat continued to be too expensive, and many fruits were confined to southern Europe. As in previous times, the periodic bad harvests created famines which reduced the poorest peasants to eating straw, roots, rats and tree bark.

The merits of one type of bread versus another were vigorously debated. Wheat bread remained the first choice of most, but it was always expensive. Rye was "not as nourishing as wheat and loosens the bowels a little. Barley bread is refreshing but less nourishing than wheat or rye. Oats were fed to horses, not usually to people. Rye remained the food of the poor."[33] It seems that sausages appeared in Germany at this time— pork sausages were consumed with black bread and endless helpings of soup made from cabbage, watercress and cheese or dried peas and bacon simmered in boiling water.

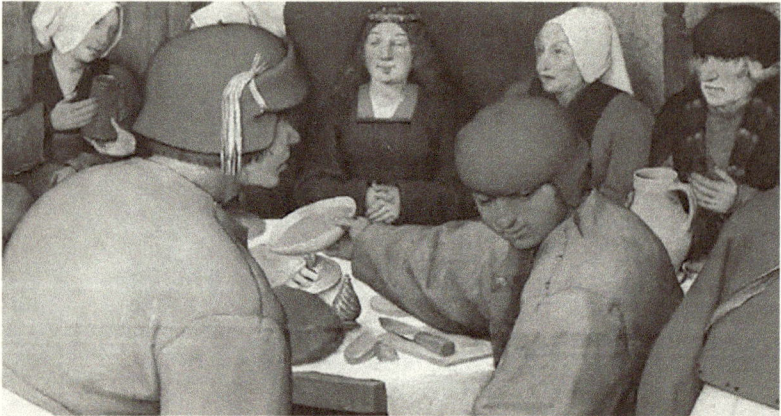

Eating habits were changing slowly.

The prosperous peasants indulged in new treats such as turkey and drinking chocolate, both introduced from Mexico. Sugar was a luxury, but when available, it was sprinkled on everything, including meat. The prosperous peasants were beginning to eat from pewter plates.

The German peasants continued to eat the same food as their ancestors—bread, porridge and soup. There were some changes in drinking habits—at least for the prosperous peasants. They began drinking water. Because of widespread contamination, safe drinking water was a luxury, but it was available. Now there were water carriers who walked the streets selling clean drinking water from wooden casks that they carried on their shoulders.[34]

The rich and poor peasants had one eating habit in common. They ate locally produced food.[35] Food did not travel well unless it was dried or salted.

This time period witnessed the first arrival of new foods from hitherto unknown places—Columbus brought back maize (corn) from his 1494 voyage, spices such as pepper, cinnamon, cloves, nutmeg and ginger—were imported after Vasco da Gama reached India by sea in 1498. Next came the Spanish conquistadores. Hernán Cortés conquered Mexico in 1520 and discovered maize. Francisco Pizarro conquered the Inca kingdom of South America in 1533 and discovered potatoes. The first sugar cane mill was opened in the Caribbean in 1503. This was the start of the so-called "Columbia Exchange," in which maize, potatoes, sweet potatoes, tomatoes and chocolate were all imported into Europe. These foods penetrated into Germany at very different rates—maize moved quickly and potatoes very slowly.[36]

The period of 1450 to 1650 was also when cod became common in the diets of Germans living in the Baltic seaports. The Hanseatic League had its capital in Lubeck, and dried cod was imported into the German ports first from the shores of Sweden, then from the shores of the Lofoten Islands (of Norway) and finally from the coast of Nova Scotia. Once it was dried, it lasted for a very long time.

Technology

This period witnessed the introduction of several new technologies. Perhaps the four most impactful were:

1. The thesis of the heliocentric universe.
2. The flintlock musket.
3. The telescope.
4. The compound microscope.

Since ancient times, it was believed that the earth was the center of the universe. This was the Ptolemaic system devised by Claudius Ptolemy in 150. Nicolaus Copernicus studied the skies, and he concluded that this theory was wrong. He decided that the sun was the center of the universe, and the earth and other planets revolved around the sun. It is widely noted that Copernicus came to these conclusions about twenty years before he published them in 1543, the year of his death. Whether he delayed because he feared ridicule or feared the wrath of the Roman Catholic Church, we will never know. In any case, this heliocentric theory was not widely accepted for another one hundred and fifty years. Copernicus argued that each planet revolved around the sun in a perfectly circular revolution, and this did not explain the planets' movements. It was only much later that historians looked back on this event and began calling it the "Copernican Revolution" and gave Copernicus credit for launching the Scientific Revolution (1550–1700).

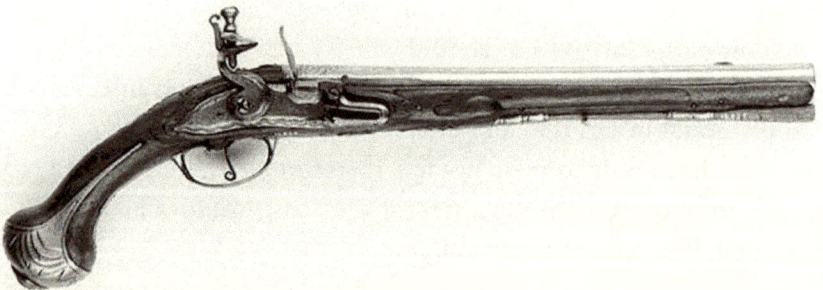

The flintlock handgun could be fired every fifteen seconds.

The flintlock firing mechanism was invented in 1600. It used a rotating disk of flint that made a spark, which immediately fired the musket. The benefit was the speed of firing multiple shots. The flintlock vastly increased the speed over the earlier "matchlock" firing mechanism where the soldier needed to strike a match and light the powder as if he were firing a baby-sized, handheld cannon. The improvement in firing speed was dramatic. It increased from once every six minutes to once every fifteen seconds.

In 1610, Galileo Galilei ground his own lenses and made a compound telescope with a magnifying power of 10x. His invention was an improvement on a simple spyglass that had been introduced a few years earlier with a magnifying power of only two or three. Galileo turned his new telescope to the sky, and there he discovered that Jupiter had moons revolving around it. He soon improved his telescope to provide 30x magnifying power.

Galileo made his own telescope in 1610.

When Galileo witnessed the movement of the moons of Jupiter, he recognized that the church's teaching that the universe was immutable was wrong. This pushed him to accept the heliocentric solar system of Copernicus. Of course, it would be many years before a German peasant would peer at the stars through a telescope, but Galileo's new technology opened wide the door for astronomers everywhere.

The invention of the compound microscope was another major breakthrough. In about 1575, the Dutch father-son team of Hans and Zacharias Janssen invented the so-called compound microscope.[37] They discovered that if they put a lens at the top and the bottom of a tube and looked through it, objects on the other end became magnified. This produced magnification of only 3x to 9x, and the images were blurry, but it laid the groundwork for future improvements. In the late 1600s, the lenses were improved to produce sharp images with as much as 270x magnifying power. These new microscopes allowed Robert Hooke to publish his book *Micrographia* in 1667, describing the cells of plants, and subsequently to be called the father of cellular biology.

Other technological breakthroughs were the Mercator projection, the slide rule, the graphite pencil, bottled beer, blood transfusions, the first primitive thermometer and the knitting machine.

The Mercator map projection was the invention of the Flemish geographer and mapmaker Gerardus Mercator. In a conventional world map, Greenland appeared to be larger than Africa, although, in reality, Africa's area is fourteen times that of Greenland. He wanted to find a way to make a two-dimensional map that did not distort the size of Greenland and other planetary landmasses that were located near the north or south pole. In 1569 he produced his solution—a map with cut-out portions like segments of an orange that displayed objects in their proportionate size. This was a breakthrough that facilitated mapmaking of the polar regions for future mapmakers. The slide rule was invented in England in 1622 after the logarithmic scales (upon which slide rules are based) had already been devised. The "lead" pencil was invented in 1564 when a huge graphite (black carbon) mine was discovered in England. The pure graphite was sawn into sheets and then cut into square rods and inserted into hand-carved wooden holders, thus forming pencils.[38] The

English had a monopoly on the production of pencils since no other pure graphite mines were known at the time.

Bottled beer came into existence in 1568. Glass bottles had been made in Germany since about 1000, and beer was much older, but they were not combined until Dr. Alexander Nowell, a Church of England rector, poured some homemade brew into a bottle, corked it and went fishing. He forgot the bottle until several days later when he returned to find the bottle still filled with beer.[39] Commercial bottling of beer probably began around 1650.

In England in 1628, Dr. William Harvey discovered that blood circulates through the human body. This caused several attempts at blood transfusions. The first attempts produced success at transfusing blood from one dog to another. Both dogs survived. Successful human transfusions had to wait.

In 1589, William Lee invented a "stocking frame," which was a knitting machine to produce stockings. He demonstrated the machine to Queen Elizabeth I, who refused to authorize a patent because she feared the effects on hand-knitting workers. Although it was a commercial failure, it served as a model for machines of the Industrial Revolution two hundred years later.

How they dressed

Clothing styles changed regularly for the nobility and even for the emerging middle class, but from 1450 to 1650, the German peasants' dress changed very little. Again, during this time, many people didn't have a change of clothes. They wore the same outfit day after day. The lack of fresh, clean clothes was the cause of many common skin diseases. In 1500, clothing served as a uniform; your clothes designated your status. Lepers were now required to wear grey outfits and red hats. Prostitutes were now required to wear red skirts. Jews were required to wear a garment with a large yellow circle. Public penitents would wear white robes. A very useful status designation for young unmarried women was the traditional velvet bands that they wore around their hair to indicate that they were not yet attached. Men continued wearing the tight-fitting hose that had been introduced about 1350.

Buttons made it possible to make form-fitting clothes.

As for women, their bodices too became more close-fitting and were cut with a large décolleté. This was another cause for censure. The shapeless, loose tunic was replaced by a two-piece outfit for the women consisting of a skirt and a blouse. The skirt was tied tightly around the waist—usually with an apron that tied in the back. The effect was to call attention to the attractive shape of the woman's small waist compared to her shapely bosom. Men also exhibited more of their bodies by wearing short jackets that displayed their legs wrapped in hose. To visualize men's hose, picture a man wearing long underwear. The codpiece continued to be worn by some men. This was a strange accessory because it was a "representation of the male sexual organ stylized in cloth and exaggeratedly large."[40]

Women wore aprons at this time. The apron was large, covering almost their entire dress, or they often wore two aprons—the inner apron was a neck to knee covering, and the outer apron was smaller, covering the waist to the knees.

Footwear became more diverse. The standard footwear for men and women was wooden clogs. Men also wore sandals or low shoes made from leather. Knee-high boots with a turned-down top became common for peasant men in the 1520s.

Hats were very popular with men and women. They came in all shapes and sizes, ranging from knitted wool caps to broad-brimmed straw hats. Men often wore hoods. (Think of a present-day "hoodie" sweatshirt.) Women also had a wide variety of hat choices, including the "capelet," which was a simple cloth covering wrapped around the head. Apparently, the common pocket was still unknown at this time. Both men and women continued to wear a pouch attached to a belt at their waist.

Peasants began to wash their clothes weekly. Wash day in the German lands required a peasant woman to boil the clothes, beat them, rinse them and then hang them out to dry or lay them in the sun to bleach.[41]

Bathing and grooming

Beginning in about 1450, we see some new additions to the bathing and grooming habits of the German peasants. An all too typical grooming activity of the day was picking lice, such as illustrated in the woodcut of the woman picking lice from her husband's hair. This period witnessed the appearance of handkerchiefs. We know that they were in existence because Erasmus wrote about them in his 1530 book entitled *De civilitate morum puerilium* (*On Good Manners for Children*). He advised, "To wipe the nose on the cap or sleeve belongs to rustics; to wipe the nose on the arm or elbow to pastry cooks, and to wipe the nose with the hand, if by chance at the same instant you hold it to your gown is not much more civil. But to receive the excreta of the nose with a handkerchief turning slightly away from noble people is an honest thing."[42]

A woodcut shows a woman picking lice from her husband's hair.

As the German people slowly migrated to the towns and cities, the public bathhouse became more common in this period. The descriptions suggest that it was not simply a utilitarian way to clean oneself. Rather it was an indulgence. It was a relaxing place for men and women to soak in hot water together and socialize. The bathers were usually entertained with some music, and they could order something to drink. It was a place to engage one of the young masseuses to provide a massage—either invigorating or calming. We can assume that it was an extravagance, which suggests that our peasant ancestors indulged only occasionally. It is interesting to note that public baths were popular only in Germany—not in France or England. In Russia and Scandinavia, they preferred saunas.

Men and women enjoying the public bathhouse together.

Travel and transportation

Between 1450 and 1650, there were some important changes in travel and transportation, especially in the design of ships that made possible the "Age of Exploration." The major innovation in land travel was the introduction of the four-wheeled cart. It quickly replaced the two-wheeled carts for hauling lumber, grain and other freight.

The four-wheel carts were a huge improvement. First, they were balanced. That is, they did not tip forward when detached from a horse. Second, the four-wheeled design led to larger versions carrying much greater loads. Four-wheel carts carried not only freight but also poor passengers.[43] Four-wheel wagons were made in various sizes, but the four-ton wagon became the typical size for use on farms.[44]

You might wonder why the four-wheeled cart was not invented until after 1450. The answer is the cart was waiting for a pivoting front axle that would allow the front axle to turn to the right or left. Some nameless person designed a pivoting mechanism. Four-wheeled carts were initially invented to pull heavy gun carriages, and they were first employed for civilian travel in 1470.[45]

While the open four-wheel cart was a significant breakthrough by itself, the four-wheel design was also revolutionary because it served as the basis for a series of other vehicles that evolved into open stagecoaches and then to enclosed stagecoaches. This period introduced the first open carriages to transport people from place to place.

Roads were improved, and more stone bridges were built to span streams and rivers. But the energy for all of this travel came either from the wind (for ships) or from horsepower or human power. The truly revolutionary changes would not come until the steam engine in the 1800s and the internal combustion engine of the 1900s.

We saw that the two major problems with travel in the previous period were mud and poor roads. They remained persistent problems. "Until the 1700s, overland transport went at a snail's pace."[46] We are told that Europe began to establish an enormous network of efficient roads in the 1200s. In a painting by Jan Breughel from the 1600s of the flat open country, "the road was not a clearly delineated strip along which traffic flowed smoothly. The holes in the road are full of water, the horsemen are squelching along, their mounts up to their hocks in water, the carriages move painfully forward, their wheels sunk in the mud. Pedestrians and pigs have wisely retired to the safer banks bordering the road."

The first primitive carriages did not offer public transportation until about 1550.[47] This was another important milestone because it marked the birth of the stagecoach business. The first stagecoaches were open to the elements. Gradually there appeared covered carriages, and then a little later, they were equipped with glass windows.

Other changes in travel came slowly. Walking remained the typical mode of transportation for peasants, although now we hear of peasants riding donkeys. Of course, the nobles continued to ride horses.

The most significant changes in transport in this period took place on the water with new ship designs. One of the most important was the "carrack." The carrack was a deep-hulled sailing ship with three or more sails that used a combination of square-rigged sails along with one lateen-rigged sail. The lateen sail usually flew from the mizzenmast, which is the mast immediately to the stern of the mainmast. The advantage of the lateen sail is that it allows the ship to sail at an angle into the wind. Perhaps the most important carrack of this time period was the Santa Maria, the flagship that took Columbus across the Atlantic in his first voyage to America in 1492. The ship was small—only fifty-eight feet long, but it was deep and sturdy (100 tons displacement), and it used three sails with a lateen rigging on the mizzenmast. These sailing ships were state of the art during the Age of Exploration (defined as 1450 to 1600).

This illustrates the new triangular lateen sail employed during the Age of Exploration to sail into the wind.

Compasses were used, and the "log and line" method was used to determine the ship's speed. This was a wooden board attached with a long line thrown from the stern of the boat. The rope was knotted at seven-fathom intervals. (A fathom is six feet, so seven fathoms equals forty-two feet.) They counted the knots that unraveled during the course of a half a minute as measured by an hourglass, enabling them to calculate the speed at which the ship was moving through the sea. This system of measurement coined the phrase "knots" as a way to measure speed in sea travel. This also enabled them to calculate the distance the ship traveled in a specific direction. These numbers were carefully written in the ship's logbook.[48]

At night they could calculate their north-south position by viewing the stars. That gave them their latitude position. The longitude calculation was a challenging problem—so difficult that the government of England offered a huge reward for anyone who could solve the problem. It was not solved until 1773, when John Harrison invented an extremely accurate chronometer (clock).

Table talk: Building a new four-wheeled cart

It is a Sunday in October of 1480 in the small town of Hochstadten in central Germany at the Muller household. The family has returned from church and finished their noon-time meal. At the table are the parents Ehrhart and Bechte Muller, and their two children Johannes aged seventeen and his younger sister, Gude.

Ehrhart is exhausted after a long week of work harvesting grain from his fields and the fields of the local lord of the manor. Their small two-wheel cart has made many trips between the fields and the barn with the horse pulling in the harvest.

Johannes is the first to speak, "Mom and Dad, I wanted to tell you about my visit to Frankfurt. You know that I delivered some grain there last week, and I happened to see one of the four-wheel carts that people have been talking about."

Ehrhart looks up from the table, "You saw a cart with four wheels?"

Johannes: "Yes." He arranged a few small sticks on the table to indicate two pairs of wheels arranged together. "In addition to the regular two wheels, this cart had a pair of wheels lined up in front, and the bed of the wagon was placed over all four wheels so that it was balanced."

Bechte: "What is so special about that?"

Johannes: "This wagon had a much bigger bed. I think it could carry two or three times as much as our two-wheel cart."

Gude is a clever young girl, and she doesn't want to be left out of this discussion, so she inserts, "I bet that would be fewer trips back and forth to the barn."

Now her father, Ehrhart, smiles for the first time. He loves his clever daughter. She is always quick to see the point. "Of course. That would be a huge benefit."

Now Gude has some momentum, so she continues, "Johannes, you are good with your hands. You seem to be able to fix anything. You could add a pair of wheels and make our wagon larger."

Johannes: "Well, it's not quite that easy. There is a reason that we have had nothing but two-wheel carts until recently."

Ehrhart: "What's that?"

Johannes: "It is the problem of that front axle."

Ehrhart: "What's the problem?"

Johannes: "The front axle has to be able to turn to the left and to the right so that the cart can turn corners."

Ehrhart: "Yes, I can see that. That is a problem? What is the solution?"

Johannes: "That's what I wanted to explain. When I was in Frankfurt, I crawled around to examine this four-wheel cart. I saw how the wheels are attached to the front axle exactly the same way as they are attached to the rear axle. The difference is that the entire front axle has to turn. Instead of always pointing straight forward, the front axle must pivot and turn to the left and to the right. This means it is attached only in the middle of the axle to the bottom of the wagon. Now it needs to be connected firmly to the wagon bottom but at the same time easy to turn."

Now Bechte remarks: "That sounds very complicated."

Johannes: "It's not too complicated. The axle needs to rotate just like the wheels of the cart need to be able to rotate."

Ehrhart: "Yes, but the difference is that you have all that weight of the wagon pressing down on the front axle, and that will make turning difficult."

Johannes: "That's right. But the key is to make the surfaces that rub against each other as smooth as possible."

Ehrhart: "Sure, that makes sense."

Johannes: "There is one more key to the pivoting. You use grease such as animal fat."

Ehrhart: "Yes, just like I grease the two wheels of my two-wheel cart to keep them turning without screeching."

Johannes: "That's it exactly. Now here is what I am going to do. Father, your birthday is on All Saints Day. This year for your birthday, I am going to build you a new four-wheeled cart. I am sure I can do it. Your four-wheel cart will be the talk of the town."

Bechte immediately thinks of their neighbor Peter who is always bragging about having the best of everything, and she smiles, "Oh, won't Peter be envious!"

Family

Because many people did not know how old they were, it is very difficult for a historian accurately to report typical marriage ages. We do, however, have one report that in the 1500s, girls married at about twenty years of age and boys at about twenty-four or twenty-five. This same source reports that between 1650 and 1700, the marriage age was delayed a little to twenty-five and twenty-seven, respectively.[49] In the absence of effective contraception, a delay in the age of marriage resulted in a lower birth rate.

Martin Luther certainly had his own views on marriage. In fact, he married a nun from a cloister that was being closed. He argued that family life was superior to celibacy. He declared that marriage created healthy bodies and consciences and protected property and honor.[50]

Girls expected to get married, and they became worried if they were not married when they reached their mid-twenties. A single woman who never married was considered useless by society. She probably was consigned to spend her days working at a spinning wheel and being called a "spinster."[51]

One source reports that the average number of surviving children rose from 2.9 in the 1540s to 3.5 in the 1590s.[52] Grandparents or other relations may have lived nearby and contributed help but rarely dwelt beneath the parental roof. Children born outside marriage were probably unusual. In the sixteenth century, when illegitimate birth rates were first measured, it was never more than about 4.5 percent.

In the 1500s, the father continued to rule the family and often arranged marriages for each of his children.[53] Poorer people continued to marry later than the rich, and the poor had fewer children. It became more common for older people to prepare a contract in which they gave the property to their children with the proviso that the children would take care of their parents until they died.

Babies continued to be quickly baptized so that if the baby died, the soul would go straight to heaven. There were no birth certificates resulting in adults not knowing their date of birth. Most peasant children continued to receive little or no education.

Table talk: Passing on the family farm

The year is 1501. It is a cold January evening, and Hette has served dinner to her two sons: Konrad is twenty-nine, and Nicolaus is twenty-three. Hette became a widow two years ago when her husband Georg died suddenly. Since then, she has been running the forty-acre Muller family farm. Her daughter Elsebeth married well several years ago to a slightly older man who had a good farm. They have two young children, and Hette dotes on her grandchildren. Hette is a strong person—fifty years old and seems to be good at everything. Her kitchen garden is the envy of the village. She makes the best butter and serves as the village healer. She is also a thoughtful, wise person. She knows that Konrad is unhappy.

Konrad has been engaged to his sweetheart, Katherine, for eight years. He can't marry Katherine until he owns the farm. But Georg bequeathed the entire property to his wife, Hette. The Muller family lives comfortably in a solid Fachwerk house. The two sons do most of the fieldwork on the large farm, supplemented by a hired man.

Hette has prepared a will and left the entire farm to her older son, Konrad. Both her parents lived into old age, and Hette hopes to do the same. But she knows what is eating away at Konrad. He wants to take over the farm because he wants to marry Katherine now. He has been engaged for eight years. Katherine is also getting impatient, and other suitors are paying attention to her.

Hette has given the situation a good deal of thought and has decided to face the issue head on. She has quietly invited Katherine to come over after dinner, and now she hears a knock at the door.

Konrad is surprised when he sees his mother invite Katherine to join them. He looks at both his mother and Katherine and asks, "What's this?"

Hette: "Konrad, you are unhappy. I understand that. You want to marry Katherine. I understand that too. And you would like to run the farm yourself. I can't blame you. I asked Katherine to join us to discuss a possible solution."

Konrad is now embarrassed and resentful. There are times that he wishes his mother were dead so that he could get on with his life, but then he is filled with remorse as well as resentment. Now his mother has invited Katherine to join in looking at this family dilemma. He clams up and stares at his mother.

Hette continues. She is strong and confident but also sensitive. She begins by addressing both Konrad and Katherine, "I can imagine it is very hard for the two of you to keep postponing your wedding. I was engaged to Georg for six months, and those were the longest months of my life."

She smiles at her son and Katherine. Invoking her beloved husband softens both of them. They both relax a little.

Hette continues, "Katherine, you are the princess of the village. Konrad is very fortunate to have won your love. But you must be eager to get married."

Now it is Katherine's turn. She is also a strong woman who speaks her mind. "You're right, Hette. I am now twenty-six. I very much want to get married and start raising children. I am ready."

Now Konrad speaks up, "Mother, you can't blame me for wanting to take over the farm."

Hette says, "Konrad, I don't blame you for a moment, but you can see that we have something of a dilemma here. This is my farm. This house is my house. I love doing what I do, and I am good at it. We have all prospered. I have thought of turning over the farm to you, but then this house will become yours and Katherine's. You will have children. I will be in the way."

Katherine starts to say something, but Hette holds up her hand and continues, "I know you would both try to make me a welcome guest, but Katherine, you are a strong person. You are an excellent cook. You would want to take charge of the house and cook the meals and tend your own kitchen garden and not have a mother-in-law looking over your shoulder."

Katherine knows this is true. She loves and respects Hette, and she refuses to try to fool her. So she nods at Hette and says, "You're right, Hette. Just as Konrad wants to run a farm of his home, so I would like a house of my own."

Hette is actually pleased with the progress of this conversation. She has dealt with the hard part—getting them both to admit that they would like to take over the farm and the house. Now she moves to her proposal.

Hette says, "I have an offer for both of you. Suppose you agreed to build me a new house subject to my approval—a smaller house of course, but a house here in the village where I can entertain my friends and enjoy my grandchildren. I would also expect a certain monthly payment for my living expenses. This farm does very well. The payments should not be a problem. If we could agree to that, I would deed the farm over to you, Konrad, and I would move to this new house so that you, Katherine, could have this place as your home. How does that sound?"

Konrad and Katherine look at each other. It is exactly the kind of arrangement that Katherine had imagined but was reluctant to share with Konrad. But Konrad is frowning.

Katherine knows Konrad better than he knows himself, so she speaks next. "That is a wonderfully generous offer, Hette. Do you think you would be happy giving up this fine house?"

Hette: "Oh, yes. I will have plenty to keep me busy. I will create a garden behind my new house. I will have an extra room to have my grandchildren sleep over. I will have time to work with my herbs for my healing work. And I will be happy seeing you and Konrad married."

That final statement was what broke through Konrad's resentment. He turned to his mother, "Mother, I don't exactly know what to say. . . ."

Hette steps in again, "Don't say anything right away. It is a big decision for each of us. Take a little time to think it through and discuss it with Katherine. We can get together again next week, and if you agree to the plan, you can start planning your wedding."

Now the three all smile at each other.

Health and medical care

The major health issue for this period was the spread of various infectious diseases. Syphilis broke out in 1493 in Naples among French soldiers fighting against the Spanish army for control of Naples. It spread across Europe and was known as "the French disease." It was extremely virulent from 1493 to about 1700.[54] After 1650, syphilis was treated with mercury taken internally and externally along with extreme heat in steam baths.[55] Typhus and smallpox both increased around 1500.[56] One version of smallpox was especially deadly with mortality rates of 25 percent.

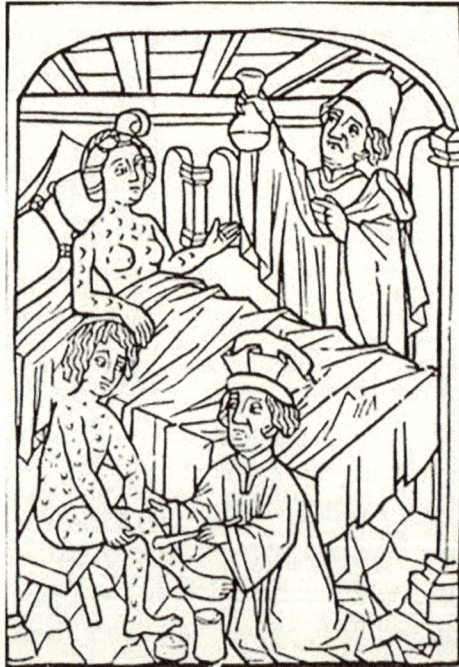

From about 1493 to about 1700, there were repeated syphilis epidemics.

This was also the time of certain deficiency diseases. Scurvy was the classic shipboard disease. It was triggered by a deficiency of vitamin C (ascorbic acid). Scurvy is an old disease, but it takes thirty weeks of vitamin C deprivation for the symptoms to appear. The symptoms start with spongy, bleeding gums followed by open wounds and eventually death. Because there were few voyages of thirty weeks before 1500, it was a rare disease. The Age of Discovery involved long voyages, and this brought out the age of scurvy.[57] The diagnosis and antidote would have to wait until 1750.

Barber shops performed surgeries, including pulling teeth. There were no antibiotics, and infections were often fatal. Barbers were also engaged to saw off an infected leg. Remember, there were no painkillers. Barbers also removed lice from the scalp.[58]

Let's look at some of the improved treatments and medical breakthroughs of this period. The Swiss doctor Paracelsus (1493–1541) represented a sharp break with traditional medicine. In fact, he threw the writings of Galen into a bonfire to demonstrate his rejection of the ancient "humor theory" of disease. He also rejected the popular all-purpose medicines and treatments. He believed in careful observation and interviewing the patient. He concluded that each disease was a separate thing, thus anticipating the germ theory of the 1800s. He was called the "Luther of medicine" because he rejected authority. He lectured in German, not in Latin, because he wanted to communicate with the common people. He criticized blood-letting and other heroic measures. He supported the "old women" who healed with mild herbs.[59]

In 1500 Leonardo da Vinci dissected many cadavers enabling him to publish a book entitled *Anatomy* with remarkably accurate illustrations.

A major breakthrough in medical care occurred when universities became centers for medical research and the training of doctors. Although Germany lagged behind Italy, France and England, Germany began creating universities in 1386 with Heidelberg University. In the 1400s, a series of universities were created, including Freiburg in 1457 and Tuebingen in 1477. These universities established standards, basic protocols and procedures. The universities also fostered research to discover breakthroughs in diagnosis and treatment. For example, the

University of Salerno introduced animal dissections and then slowly expanded to human dissections. Human dissections soon led to autopsies performed by surgeons to determine the actual cause of death. Gradually a university education became the standard method of qualifying to serve as a physician. A university education replaced the traditional method of a guild with its apprenticeship program.

In the 1500s, there were many wounds from firearms and gunpowder. These were treated initially with boiling oil to cauterize the wound, but in 1536, a French surgeon created a mixture of egg yolk, rose oil and turpentine. This caused the patients to suffer less and heal quicker, and it became the standard treatment for gun wounds.[60]

Without an effective anesthesia or a way to give blood transfusions, surgery was very challenging, but in the 1580s, a Swiss pig-gelder performed the first successful caesarean section in which the baby and the mother both survived. His experience and skill in using a surgeon's knife were developed in his career of castrating farm animals for a living. The mother recovered and lived to the age of 77.[61] This successful C-section was a unique achievement and was not equaled until the twentieth century made antisepsis standard.

Some effective medicines were imported from the New World. The Incas used coca leaves, the source of cocaine, as an anesthetic. They used dried seaweed which is rich in iodine as a preventative medicine against goiter.[62]

Although there were various innovations, the overall delivery of health care changed very little between 1450 and 1650. First, there were very few university-trained doctors. Most peasants would never see one. Second, the techniques of diagnosis and treatment by the "experts" were so ineffective that most people concluded that a good housewife might be more effective in providing healthy remedies than an expensive physician or surgeon.[63]

Attitudes toward mental illness were slowly evolving. In 1450 people who were viewed as mad were sometimes locked up in chains in Nuremberg, but usually they were looked after at home.[64] This was a period in which people of every walk of life were vulnerable to tooth and gum diseases. It is likely that many people lost most of their teeth. Either they fell out of diseased gums or pulled to stop toothaches. It is known that many had very bad breath—including the kings and queens. Tooth care was minimal—an occasional scrubbing with a cloth or picking between the teeth with a twig.

The ultimate measure of the quality of health care during that era is reflected in the outcomes. In 1600 life expectancy had not improved in the past one thousand years. For those born around 1600, 27 percent died before their first birthday. Another 12 percent died between ages one and four, and another 6 percent died between ages five and nine. Altogether about 45 percent of the children died before they reached the age of ten.[65] During this time, people were preoccupied with death.

Warfare and weaponry

This period brought revolutionary changes in warfare and weaponry. Offensively, the key change agent was gunpowder. Gunpowder was the key ingredient in the progressive evolution of the two revolutionary weapons: artillery and handguns. Defensively, the major change was the demise of the treasured medieval city walls—which were made obsolete by gunpowder.

Let's talk gunpowder. The Chinese invented gunpowder which was mixed in a precise recipe from saltpeter (Potassium nitrate), charcoal and sulfur.[66] The recipe calls for 75 percent saltpeter, 12.5 percent charcoal and 12.5 percent sulfur.[67] Saltpeter is an unusual material. It is a manmade substance that starts with some kind of manure high in nitrates (such as bat guano), then it is treated with additional urine and finally dried into crystals. Gunpowder and its recipe gradually arrived from China before 1450. We know it was used in Europe in 1324 during the siege of Metz in France. But gunpowder was not accepted overnight.[68] At first, it was quite expensive, which limited its appeal. Second, "the kings and knights did not immediately embrace gunpowder because their place in society was established by their ability to fight in time-honored ways with horses and swords. Even regular soldiers were reluctant to use gunpowder weapons. These weapons rattled the ground and produced terrifying roars, and therefore they seemed to be the work of Satan, not God."[69]

The breakthrough for gunpowder waited over one hundred years until the 1453 siege of Constantinople. Mehmet the Conqueror led the besieging Ottoman army that surrounded the Byzantine capital, and he ordered gigantic cannons to be built by the Hungarian engineer Orban. He delivered three of these monster cannons, which were as much as twenty-seven feet long with a barrel three feet in diameter. They could shoot a stone ball one-and-a-half miles. These cannons demolished the previously impregnable walls of Constantinople, giving the Ottomans one of the most famous military victories in world history. Suddenly the cannon and its gunpowder were king. Because of the success of these huge cannons, the initial thinking was that the bigger the cannon, the better.

Simultaneously, gunpowder was producing hand weapons that were also transformative, the first of which was the arquebus. This seems to have been the earliest handgun. It had a long, thin barrel. The inside of the barrel was smooth, so it didn't cause the bullet to spin, and the first bullets were round pieces of lead. Their problem was that they were astonishingly inaccurate. One estimate reports that only one bullet in five hundred hit its target.[70] The illustration shows a man using a tripod in an attempt to improve the accuracy of his arquebus.

The first manual firearm was the arquebus.

Accuracy would come first from a longer barrel in the form of a musket. A second improvement was cylinder-shaped bullets with more weight and less air resistance. A third improvement was "rifling," a German invention in 1498. Rifling refers to etching grooves inside the barrel of the gun to cause the bullet to spin, making it more wind-resistant and easier to aim true. Rifling improvements were made in the 1500s in Nuremberg, but it was not until the late 1800s that computations were applied to optimize rifling. Accuracy was always a challenge in the early handguns and rifles.

Both artillery and hand firearms evolved during this period. First, the cost of gunpowder began to decline in the late 1300s.[71] After 1450, both artillery and firearms evolved in interesting ways.

Artillery became smaller. A very large cannon was so heavy that it required twenty horses to move it and another forty horses and many men to transport the stone cannonballs. Soon, these large cannons were relegated exclusively for use in sieges. For actual battles, cannons became smaller, so they were more mobile. The Swedish general Gustavus Adolphus perfected the best way to use cannon in battles. He used a type of small canon that he created to shoot three-pound balls. Most importantly, it could be moved quickly by one horse and three men. For the first time, cannons could keep up with infantry on the battlefield. He used these small cannons with masterly effectiveness in the 1630s during the Thirty Years' War. Cheaper cannons were made of iron, and more expensive cannons were made of bronze with a ratio of 8 parts of tin to 92 parts of copper.[72] This was the same ratio used in casting bronze church bells.

Firearms had an even more interesting trajectory. They evolved into what we now call "rifles and revolvers." During this period, rifles became more accurate, and the improved firing mechanism made them much faster to shoot and reload. The first arquebuses probably appeared around 1475. These handguns were loaded and fired with a matchlock that required lighting the fuse with a match before each shot.[73] This was time-consuming, of course, and gradually the speeds of firing a matchlock gun increased from a shot every six minutes to a shot every one and a half minutes.

The slow firing rate made it "impossible to abandon the pike—still described as the queen of weapons—in the 1600s because arquebuses took a long time to manipulate."[74] Despite their slow firing rate, arquebuses were a critical factor in a Spanish victory over the French in 1503.[75] Handguns were cheaper to make and easier to use than the crossbow. In 1500 the wheellock became the first self-igniting firing mechanism. A steel disc rotated and provided an ignition spark. This was superseded in 1600 by the flintlock, which was faster. By 1650, the state-of-the-art long gun was a musket with a flintlock. This enabled much faster firing—with a shot every fifteen seconds. Shorter handguns also evolved, mainly to improve on the abysmal lack of accuracy of the first arquebuses.

The use of handguns and artillery not only changed the tactics of warfare but also gave the infantry (composed of peasants) superiority over the cavalry (composed of knights). This shift hastened the demise of the knights and the nobility in general, beginning around 1450.[76]

Villages had been protected with earthen and wooden walls since Neolithic times, but the golden age of the wall was from 1200 to 1450. As previously noted, during this period, walls were made of stone, and they were designed to be indestructible—usually, seven feet thick and twenty-four to forty feet high.[77] The destruction of the walls of Constantinople collapsed not only the walls but also the notion that walls were invincible. Nevertheless, walls continued to be built until about 1600. "Walls defined a city and were a source of civic pride. Large imposing walls became a sign of prosperity. Less important towns were left unwalled. These walls were financed with taxes."[78]

Another change in warfare was the increased size and complexity of the fighting forces. For example, during the Thirty Years' War (1618–1648), the commander for the Royalist/Roman Catholic side, "General Wallenstein gathered 100,000 soldiers under his command. This required exceptional logistic support. It implies that a supply train had to carry 120,000 rations a day (because some men received double rations) and this meant that a four-day supply required 480,000 rations with 800 rations transported in a single carriage. This would require 600 carriages and 2,400 horses harnessed in fours."[79]

Perils

There was a traditional prayer that was prayed again and again. "O Lord, save us from plague, famine, and war."[80] They were probably the three worst perils of the early modern age in the German lands beginning in 1450. Let's look at these three perils and then several other perils of this period.

The first peril was a very familiar threat—plague. Its cause was not understood, and so there was no effective prevention or treatment. The plague continued to return, and between 1450 and 1650, there were twelve recurrences that spread death and terror. There was a return of the plague in 1456, then 1464, next in 1481, and there were nine more events before 1650. Each time, this deadly pandemic killed thousands during a two- or three-year period.

The second of these perils, famine, was an age-old danger. Over 80 percent of the peasants were subsistence farmers. They subsisted literally from year to year. This meant that they counted on each harvest to produce enough food to get the family through the next twelve months—without touching one-quarter of the crop, which had to be saved for next year's seed. The most common cause of famine was bad weather. Sometimes there wasn't enough rain, and the crops wilted. In other cases, there was too much rain, and planting was delayed. Or it rained during harvest time, and the crops went to rot.

The 1600s brought a "little ice age" with very cold winters. These cold winters usually meant a late spring, a late planting and poor harvests. Finally, unusually cold weather could spoil a part of the harvest.

Another "Little Ice Age" began in 1600 with especially cold winters and late springs.

Starvation was a slow and relentless killer. We learn that starvation kills a healthy human in six to ten weeks. Initially, a person can lose up to 10 percent of their body weight without losing much strength or energy. After that, they begin to decline. When they have lost 15 percent to 20 percent of their normal body weight, they become depressed and apathetic and can no longer participate in day-to-day life. As a person continues to lose weight, the stomach accumulates abnormal amounts of watery fluids, and the stomach balloons outwards. Eventually, when a person has lost about 40 percent of their body mass, death is inevitable.[81]

Of course, in the process of starving, they become desperate. William Manchester reports that a poor harvest and famine came about once every four years. The hunger was terrible. The peasants would be forced to sell everything they owned, including the clothes off their backs. To buy a little food, they would be reduced to nudity.

The third major peril was war. This two-hundred-year period suffered the worst effects of any war in the German lands. The Thirty

Years' War was fought exclusively on German soil. Here is one eyewitness description: "A number of soldiers began to slaughter, to boil and roast things, while others, on the other hand, stormed through the house from top to bottom. Others made a large pack out of linens, clothes and all kinds of household goods. Everything they didn't want to take with them, they destroyed. A number of them stuck their bayonets into the straw and hay, as if they didn't have enough sheep and pigs to stick. Many of them shook out the feathers from the bedcovers and filled them with ham. Others threw meat and other utensils into it. Some knocked in the oven and the windows, smashing copper utensils and dishes. Bedsteads, tables, stools and benches were burned. Pots and cutting boards were all broken. One servant girl was so badly handled in the barn that she couldn't move any longer. Our servant they tied up and laid on the ground and rammed a funnel in his mouth and they poured a ghastly brew of piss down his throat. Then they started to torture the peasants as if they wanted to burn a bunch of witches."[82] Aside from the abstract estimates that one-third of the German population died during the war, this description paints a gruesome picture of the wanton cruelty suffered by the peasants.

Soldiers on both sides were vicious in their plundering of helpless peasants.

The Thirty Years' War brought atrocities such as hangings of innocent civilians.

There were three other perils during this period—superstitious hysteria, religious fanaticism and homicide. The years 1450 to 1650 represent a time of superstitious hysteria. When there was a calamity of some kind, some of the hysterical people looked for a scapegoat. All too often, that scapegoat became the Jewish residents of the community. In response to the Black Death of 1347–1350, the Jews were accused of causing the disease by poisoning the town wells. The rumors and accusations spread into a wave of hysteria. The hysterical Germans were known to gather together Jews into one large building, lock the doors and burn the building to the ground killing all the Jews who were trapped inside. It happened in one German community after another.[83]

Religious fanaticism expressed itself in other dangerous ways. If your beliefs were not in accord with the accepted religious doctrines of a particular community, you were labeled a "heretic." In 1494 the ultimate punishment for a heretic was to be burned at the stake.

And finally, there was always the peril of someone murdering you. If you were a young man between the ages of eighteen and thirty, you were especially vulnerable. It was a violent age. Everyone carried a knife. There was a lot of drinking. There was free-floating testosterone. In the 1520s, the homicide rate averaged seventy-five per year for every 100,000 residents.[84] (By comparison, the homicide rate in Germany today is close to one per year for every 100,000 residents.) Ninety-five percent of both the victims and perpetrators were men, and overwhelmingly they were from the eighteen to thirty age group. Let's estimate that males represented 50 percent of the population, and eighteen- to thirty-year-olds were 25 percent of the male population. This means that each year in the German lands, seventy-five out of 12,000 young men were murdered.

Worries

We have seen that in the previous period the four major worries were:

1. A return of the plague.
2. Poor crops resulting in famine.
3. How could they leave enough land so that their children could support themselves as respectable farmers.
4. Death and hell.

In 1450 the main worries had shifted a little. First, it seems likely that a recurrence of the plague remained a great worry. Indeed, there were twelve recurrences during this two-hundred-year period. On average, the plague swept through the German lands every eight years. They surely got an early warning at the first outbreak in their locality. The typical plague lasted for three years for each recurrence. So, we can imagine that when they first heard that the plague had touched a nearby town, the worry must have set in.

The second most common worry in this period concerned hell and death again, but this time it was a little more nuanced. The Church focused on the imagery of purgatory. This was a "never-never" land where people languished halfway between heaven and hell in a celestial limbo. The church developed very specific programs to reduce the time in purgatory—for a living person or for a loved one who had already died. Indulgences were a big part of this program. Indulgences were designed to offer penitents a reprieve from purgatory. It was important to have masses said on your behalf after you died to minimize one's time in purgatory and open the gates to heaven quickly. This became an obsession with many religious people. They often deeded their entire estate to the church in return for an agreement that so many masses would be said for the person languishing in purgatory to get them released from purgatory and through the gates of heaven. The selling of indulgences played right into this worry about purgatory.

Purgatory was depicted as a limbo of endless waiting.

The third worry common in this era was the survival of an expectant mother who was about to give birth. Infant mortality was approximately 20 percent for the infant. The mortality rate for the mother was about 1 percent.[85] Most of these deaths were the result of infections caused by germs. But the germ theory would not be understood until the 1800s. The death of an infant, mother, or both, seemed like a random event that happened all too frequently. A young couple with several children must have been very worried about the survival of the mother when the third child was born. Her death would be a disaster for her family—not only emotionally but practically and financially as well. In order to cope, the husband would need to find a step-mother for his children.

Fourth, there must have been many worries centered around marriage. Both the man and the woman are expected to be married. It was extremely difficult to earn a living and cope with life if you were single. The young peasants knew that a successful, happy life required two things: Owning a farm so that the couple could support themselves and being able to produce children to continue their family line. The first worry was—when will I be in a position to be married? This required the young man to have inherited the family farm. It was very common for a young man to wait until his father died. This would mean that the family farm was now in his hands. This farm provided him with the means of supporting himself and a wife and children. The young man might be engaged at age twenty-one but be forced to wait until he inherited the farm—which might not happen until he was, let us say twenty-nine.

But there was still another worry related to marriage. Each partner wondered if the partner was fertile and capable of becoming a biological parent. To ensure that the couple could conceive, they often slept together before they committed to marriage. When the young lady appeared to be pregnant, the couple's doubts would be erased, and they set a date for their wedding.

Self-image

After 1450 there was certainly a new spirit of individualism. The Reformation was largely responsible for this new awareness. Each individual had a direct relationship with God. Each was expected to serve God with an honest day's work, to teach their children about the love of God and to offer forgiveness and stand for justice. This period was also the dawn of humanism. Erasmus (1466–1536) was the "father of humanism." Almost everyone came to identify themselves as Lutherans or Catholics, Reformed or Anabaptist. Almost no one said, "I am a humanist." But the humanist spirit seeped into much of the German population after Erasmus. Humanism "opened a vista on the goals that could be reached on earth: individual self-development, action rather than pious passivity, a life in which reason and will can be used both to improve worldly conditions and to observe the lessons that nature holds for the thoughtful."[86] To some degree, this spirit of humanism began to infect Germans of all religious persuasions. But there was a long way to go before the typical German peasant felt truly empowered.

In fact, one source reports that until about "1500, most people in Europe had an almost total lack of ego. For example, we have all these magnificent Gothic cathedrals built by anonymous workers."

We are also reminded of the lack of identifying with their native country. Indeed throughout the period, the German lands were a patchwork of several hundred tiny kingdoms, so we should not be surprised. "Most people identified themselves first with the family and household, then a village or small town. They spoke a local dialect, shared in a regional culture and were only vaguely aware of the affairs of the kingdom."[87]

Finally, the Thirty Years' War was a catastrophe in the German lands, second only to the Black Death of 1348. The war's rampant destruction was random and uneven. Some parts of Germany were almost unscathed, but others were almost wiped out. In those devastated areas which witnessed thefts, killing of their livestock, burning of their crops, torture and murder, the sense of those peasants must have been something like helpless rage. Their sense of personal identity must have been filled with victimhood.

There was another crosscurrent during this period. "The Age of Exploration brought new foodstuffs and new raw materials that poured into Europe, while an awareness of far horizons also gave an incalculable stimulus to the life of the intellect and the imagination."[88]

Religion and values

The church in the German lands went through a difficult transition period after the Reformation took hold. Many churches renounced Roman Catholicism and embraced the Lutheran faith and practices. This was reinforced by the conclusion of the Thirty Years' War in 1648 when the German map was divided into Catholic areas and Protestant areas.

Certainly, some devout people moved to a different region of the German lands when the ruler of their particular kingdom established a church with which they disagreed. There must have been some measure of Protestants and Catholics moving so they could live and worship in accord with their conscience. But most of the residents gradually adopted the established faith.

In the Protestant areas, pastors married and had families. The services were no longer in Latin but in vernacular German. The sacraments were narrowed to two—baptism and communion. The Protestant churches continued to collect the tithe—a 10 percent tax on each peasant. But none of the money was funneled to Rome. Instead, the money was used locally to pay the minister and support other church work—possibly running a hospital or feeding the hungry.

The majority of the Protestants were Lutherans. The Lutheran Church allowed and encouraged pastors to marry and have children. The church ministers who could not or would not convert to the Lutheran denomination were often sent away to live out their years together in a monastery confiscated from the Roman Catholic Church. Lutherans continued some of the high liturgies of the Catholic Church. But now, the services were in vernacular German. The congregation began to join in the singing during worship. Luther wrote hymns for the new hymnbooks. Birth control was not prohibited. Families became smaller.

It should be remembered that the Roman Catholic Church continued to teach that sex was approved by God only if it was for the purpose of creating children. Birth control was prohibited. Recreational sex was still forbidden. Masturbation was deemed worse than adultery.

The second-largest Protestant group was the Reformed Church, founded by Ulrich Zwingli in Switzerland. John Calvin later led it before being imported to Scotland under John Knox as the Presbyterian Church.

This denomination was suspicious of religious paintings and statues in churches. Their churches were plain and barren. John Calvin also taught that making loans and charging interest was permissible if the interest rates were reasonable.

Some of the doctrinal disputes were technical. For instance, the Lutheran Church taught the "real presence" of Jesus Christ in the celebration of communion. The reformed church said the celebration was simply symbolic and should be performed only four times a year. The reformed famously taught the doctrine of predestination. Each human was preordained either to believe in Jesus Christ and be saved or to reject Jesus Christ and be condemned. As part of this doctrine, the church taught that there were certain signs in one's earthly life that indicated whether or not you were among the saved. The principal sign was that you lived a sober and industrious life. This teaching was combined with the permission to lend money at interest to motivate church members to work hard, invest their money prudently, and live modestly without ostentation.

In 1905 the German sociologist Max Weber wrote an influential book called *The Protestant Ethic and the Spirit of Capitalism.* He argued that it was the religious orientation of these followers of Calvin that translated into their habits of industriousness, saving money and investing prudently. These were all ingredients of the capitalist boom that was on the horizon.

Prior to the Reformation, the people who had money were almost always large landholders born into the nobility. The mindset of most of the nobility was to spend their money on themselves and on entertaining. There was no great motivation for saving and investing. The Reformed Church changed mindsets, and countries that were dominated by the church—Switzerland, Holland, Scotland and parts of Germany—slowly became renowned for their prosperity.

The third-largest group of Protestants was the Anabaptist group. This was never a monolithic group but rather a collection of independent sects. At the outset, they differentiated themselves by their belief in adult baptism. They believed that to become a Christian, one needed to be reborn in a spiritual sense. The key to this rebirth was personal faith. You could not be baptized as an infant into the church with the assumption that now you were counted among the "saved." Instead, each person must make a personal decision and lifelong commitment to follow Jesus Christ. Then they would be baptized with total immersion in a lake or river to signify this life-changing event.

The leaders of this movement in the 1500s were infamous for undergoing rebaptism. (Hence the label Anabaptist, which means "again baptized.") What is worth noting is that this Anabaptist spirit served as the foundation for the various Baptist denominations that appeared as well as the Amish and the Mennonites. The donations of their members financed these churches since they were not eligible for the revenues of the tithe that the government imposed.

Just as the Catholics had persecuted the Protestants, so these radical reformers who taught adult baptism were also persecuted, found guilty of heresy and sometimes burned at the stake by the mainline Protestant authorities.

Laws and political institutions

In this section, let's examine how the German lands became fragmented into hundreds of tiny kingdoms and why each village carefully determined who had the right to be a "burger" of that village.

We know that in the 1500s, the German lands continued to be fragmented into hundreds of separate territories. These were fiefdoms ruled by a knight or other nobleman and not subject to any overrule except for the nominal control of the emperor himself. The fiefdoms were hereditary. Here is how these fiefdoms were created.

Frederick I (nicknamed "Barbarossa because of his red beard") was the Holy Roman Emperor in the 1100s. During his reign, he built several castles and then deeded over these castles to various noblemen to administer on his behalf.[89]

This act of building a castle and giving it and surrounding land to a nobleman helps explain how the German lands were carved into many small "kingdoms." An imperial knight might be given a parcel of land, and now this land would remain in his family. It was passed on to the oldest son from generation to generation as a noble inheritance. The knights eventually joined together in a voluntary federation. In 1599 there were about seventy-five knights ranging from prosperous to poverty-stricken who belonged to the confederation. The average size of their individual territories was less than fourteen square miles, but these territories were true kingdoms. These lands were not part of any larger kingdom but were independent "countries." The respective lords were in control of their country or kingdom. They answered to no overlord except to the emperor himself. Since the emperor was far away and there were so many of these small kingdoms, this effectively meant that the knight ran the kingdom with a free hand.

No doubt the knights looked back nostalgically at their heyday in the medieval period when they held real power and prestige, but by the 1500s, their military skills were no longer needed. Nonetheless, the territories that they ruled were not taken away. Instead, they became anachronisms, but they endured until the Napoleonic invasions of the early 1800s.

This means that until 1800 the German lands were a hodgepodge of "kingdoms" large and small. The largest were Brandenburg-Prussia, Hanover, Saxony, Bavaria and the Rhineland Palatinate. A powerful noble ruled these five kingdoms and served as an "elector" who voted for the next Holy Roman Emperor. In addition to these five secular kingdoms, there were three ecclesiastical electorates of similar rank—Mainz, Cologne and Trier. The respective bishops were also "electors." Next in rank were smaller kingdoms such as Hessen-Darmstadt and Braunschweig-Wolfenbutel. At the very bottom of the pecking order were the tiny independent holdings of the imperial knights we described above.

Gradually the cities, towns and villages established a roll of "burgers" to define exactly who was granted the rights and privileges of being a citizen of that community. Based on the "good old law" of Germanic custom, the lord of the kingdom would establish a web of obligations for the citizens. The lord controlled all the land and owned most of it. In return, he was obligated to provide military protection for his citizens as well as help villagers through years of bad harvest and other disasters.

As a practical matter, the citizens of the village owned much of the land in common—meadows, pastures and forests. This land was shared by all the villagers who enjoyed citizen rights. Some peasant families owned their farmland outright, but "they were still obligated to pay the local lord a death tax when the head of the family died. Sometimes the local lord set the death tax so high that the surviving family members were forced to settle the debt by turning over the land to the local lord and agreeing to become his serfs.

The peasants always had to deal with tax collectors.

Conditions were the harshest in parts of the eastern and northern German lands, where lords did not rent out the land for tenants to farm but instead farmed the land themselves, using the peasants as laborers without any claim to the land itself.[90]

Crime and punishment

The 1500s were the age of the sword, which was usually wide and short.[91] Many men carried a sword as well as a knife during this century. In the 1500s, one's head was . . . the symbolic center of one's manliness. This is why serious quarrels could break out when someone pulled the hair, even worse, the beard, of another even in jest.[92]

It was easy to escape the consequence of one's crimes. Punishment in Europe was harsh but rarely enforced. In one community, two out of three culprits fled and 4 percent joined the army to enjoy immunity as long as they were in military service. Only 12 percent were imprisoned. There remained a tolerance for those who killed another human being.[93] In the illustration, we see a man on horseback. That alone signaled that he was either a nobleman or a prosperous peasant. He was easy prey for a band of "outlaws" hiding out in the woods.

Bandits were a ubiquitous part of a violent age.

For several reasons, judicial reform swept Europe around 1650. The Thirty Years' War ended in 1648, and most of Europe, especially the German lands, had been exposed to horrific violence, bloodshed and cruelty. The reform was a reaction against the scars of this violence. This coincided with the gathering strength of the Age of Absolutism (1550–1800), in which the European kings and princes were committed to demonstrate their control over society. Homicide and infanticide were singled out as the worst kind of crimes, and punishment was often a death sentence. The kings and princes saw it as their royal duty to keep the peace and enforce the Biblical injunctions against taking another life. Rulers concluded that they ruled by divine right, and they alone had the divine right over life and death. In contrast, non-aggravated theft was treated much more leniently.[94] But this would change in the 1700s.

Judicial torture peaked in usage between 1500 and 1650 when it was used not as a punishment per se but rather as a means to extract a confession when the authorities were convinced the accused was guilty.

Executions were public and became major dramatic events. Drama of any kind was popular. Remember, this was the age of Shakespeare (1564–1616). The executions were usually by hanging, and they were announced in advance and took place in the market square. People of all classes gathered to witness the event. Usually, the condemned person (almost always a man) was given a chance to speak. It was expected that he would repent and warn the audience not to follow his example. This was designed to use the punishment as a deterrent to others. In those rare cases, when the condemned was not repentant, they cut out his tongue so he could not give an impious or rebellious speech. The event was meant to signify that the king (or prince) was the sole dispenser of justice and had a monopoly on the killing of human beings.[95]

The hysteria of burning "witches" peaked between 1560 and 1670.

Ancient Germanic beliefs in ghosts and the vengeance of the dead were the basis for the German custom of mutilating the body. This was the basis for decapitating a corpse, dismembering a body or leaving the corpse on a public gibbet. In extreme cases, the body was literally torn apart by the "breaking wheel." All of these measures prevented the possibility of a return of the ghost as well as prevented a resurrection at the time of the Last Judgment.[96]

At this time across Europe, the towns were surrounded by rings of corpses and human remains—bodies hanging from the gibbet, exposed and perhaps partly burned or on a wheel, heads stuck on pikes, and severed hands. All of this display was designed to discourage bandits from passing through the gates and to reassure the inhabitants in troubled times.[97]

It was easy for a landlord to create and announce new laws and punishments in his domain in the late 1400s. For example, the barons of Gemmingen posted a notice one day in the village of Fuerfeld.[98] This notice covered several dozen laws, and it included the following:

- Excessive gambling is prohibited. Anyone who engages in dice, cards, or any other game is not allowed to bet more than a pfennig. Anyone who exceeds a daily total of 15 Kreuzer a day will be fined five shillings.

- In the past, it has been customary for villagers in the autumn to graze their livestock in the Herrschaftwoods on fallen acorns and beechnuts. This practice is now strictly forbidden.

- Clandestine marriages. i.e., entered into without the blessing of the Freiherr or the pastor, will result in corporal punishments, fines and time in the tower.

- Anyone who takes down a straight, well-growing tree from the Herrschaft woods or the community woods will be assessed a fine of three Pfunds.

The list of new laws must have seemed arbitrary to the local peasants, and it probably reinforced their sense of frustration and anger.

The early modern era in Europe was a time of the witch craze. The victims in Germany were almost always women, usually lower class, single women and often widows. If they aroused any suspicion, they were vulnerable to being accused of being a witch. They were accused of exercising supernatural powers in consort with the devil. The peak years were from 1560 to 1670. During this period, there were fifty thousand trials for witchcraft in the Holy Roman Empire (mostly in the German lands), resulting in about thirty thousand executions. Most were burned at the stake.

The witch hunt craze got so bad that a French philosopher Jean Bodin insisted that anyone who refused to believe in witches should be burned at the stake.[99] Wurzburg was a hotbed of witchcraft trials, but in 1630 Bishop Philip Adolf von Ahrenberg found both himself and his chancellor accused of witchcraft. This had gone too far. The bishop prohibited any further trials in his diocese and established regular memorial services for the innocent victims of these witch hunts.[100]

Language and literacy

Let's begin by debunking a popular misunderstanding, namely, that before the printing press appeared in 1450, almost no Germans could read and after 1450, everyone started reading. Even before the printing press, there was a small core of Germans who read—there were the monks and priests who read Latin, and there were the shopkeepers, peddlers, traders and bookkeepers who read basic German. We also are told that in 1600, one hundred and fifty years after the appearance of the printing press, only 24 percent of all Germans could read. We should remember that books printed on paper were much less expensive than those copied by hand on vellum, but they were not cheap. The twelve-hundred-page Gutenberg Bible released in 1454 was priced at 30 Florins which was three years of wages for a typical clerk at that time.

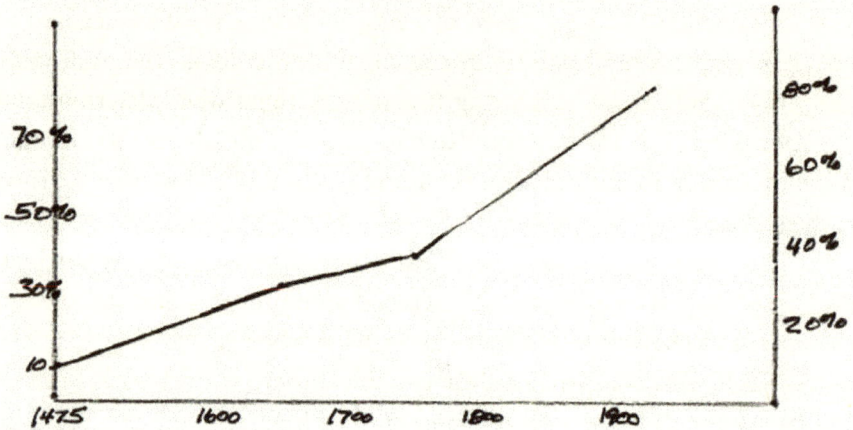

The literacy rate in the German lands increased steadily from 10 percent in 1475 to 80 percent in 1900.

Martin Luther was the driver of a modest increase in literacy in two ways. First, he translated the New Testament into German in 1522, followed by the Old Testament in 1534. In 1350 the predominant German dialect shifted into what became known as Early New High German. This was spoken south of an east-west line drawn from Aachen to Frankfurt on the Oder River. Low German was spoken north of his line, which included present-day Berlin, Hamburg and Bremen. Approximately two-thirds of Germans spoke the Early New High German.[101] Luther lived in Saxony, which was in the region of High German, and he wrote the Bible translation in his native Saxon dialect (one of the High German dialects).

Luther seemed to be aware of the importance of the language he put to print because he sought to use the vocabulary of the marketplace using simple words whenever possible. In fact, it is widely reported that Luther "made forays into nearby towns and markets in Saxony to listen to people speaking. He wanted to ensure their comprehension by translating as closely as possible to their contemporary language usage."[102] This was a major milestone because it created something for the German people to read in their own vernacular. The act of putting the Bible in print had the effect of elevating Luther's Saxon dialect to become the "standard German." Other dialects waned in importance, and some (not all) simply died out. One spoken dialect that did not die out is Swiss German. This dialect is spoken by 60 percent of the Swiss today. They call it *Schwyzerdutsch*. It is derived from a collection of Alemannic dialects that were spoken in Switzerland when Luther was translating the Bible. This dialect is the spoken language within Switzerland, but it never became a written language. Instead, the people of Switzerland had adopted Luther's Saxon dialect for reading and writing.

Second, he emphasized that each person has a direct relationship with God. They don't need an intermediary. Each person is responsible for their own beliefs, and he urged his followers to learn to read the Bible and other material (such as his religious tracts) in order to make themselves well informed. But we must be cautious when we begin to imagine that Martin Luther established schools everywhere to encourage mass literacy. That didn't happen. Indeed, the few German schools that existed tended to rely on rote learning (as schools do today in Africa, where books and writing materials are in short supply).[103]

We are fortunate to have one source reporting the overall literacy rate in various European countries from 1475 to 1900. As we see in the illustration, in 1475, it was 9 percent in the German lands—the same level as in Great Britain. The German literacy rate rose gradually; in 1550, it was 16 percent. One hundred years later, in 1650, it had almost doubled to 31 percent. These were gradual increases. It is interesting to note that another country that embraced the Lutheran faith was Sweden, where the 1475 literacy rate was less than 1 percent. It was unchanged in 1550, but then Sweden became a Lutheran country and established a mandatory education system so that all its citizens could read the Bible. By 1800 the Swedish literacy rate was almost 80 percent.

Learning to talk is intuitive. Learning to read is not. Learning to read an alphabetic language (where there is basically a different letter for each sound) requires the learner to match the symbol to the typical sound of that letter. This requires memorization. The speed of learning varies wildly. In the early 1600s, one person reported that he saw one child use a "box and wheel" device and learned the alphabet and began to read in eleven days. He noted that "slow-witted" children could take a whole year, even when beaten, to make them learn.[104]

A mother is using an alphabet board to teach her child.

We should remember that people learned to read in many different ways—some learned in school, some learned from a private tutor, but many learned from a parent, and a few others taught themselves. They sat down with a short, simple book that they had already learned by heart and began matching the letters with the sounds until they could recognize and pronounce a growing number of simple words. Children continue to teach themselves how to read today. They take a short book that they have memorized and match the sounds to the words.

What did the German people read? The newly literate Germans read the Bible in German and read "how to do it" pamphlets written by other newly literate peasants. These short manuals were known collectively as "*Kunstbuchlien*" ("skills booklets"), and they appeared throughout the German lands in the 1530s. Tens of thousands of these practical "how to do it" booklets were written in the 1500s. They explained how to throw pottery, how to make good beer, how to take good care of a horse, how to get rid of fleas and other vermin in a house, how to build a four-wheel cart with a pivoting front axle and so on.[105] What is noteworthy is that this new literacy gave birth to new peasant readers but also new peasant writers who wanted to pass along practical knowledge they had acquired.

The new double-entry bookkeeping system was useful to German bankers.

In about 150, double-entry bookkeeping appeared in the German lands. In this accounting system, there are two columns, with each entry recorded as a debit and a corresponding credit. For instance, when a merchant makes a cash payment of 100 talers, a partial repayment of his loan to his bank, the 100 talers is entered as a credit in one column to reduce the loan outstanding, and it is also entered as a debit into the column marked "Cash on hand." This new system was very useful to Jakob Fugger, the famous German banker.

At first, the printing press was devoted to printing books in Latin. The Gutenberg Bible was printed in Latin (not German) and published in 1454. In the first one hundred years, it is surprising how many books were printed in Latin, which continued to be the *lingua Franca* of Europe.

By 1500 there were 236 towns in Europe that had at least one print shop. One estimate suggests that by 1500 there were twenty million copies produced. (This assumes an average print run of one thousand copies and twenty thousand different titles.)[106]

Entertainment and simple pleasures

There certainly was a continuation of the traditional pleasures from the late Middle Ages. This included the celebrations and parties, games and dances as well as the bull-baiting and cock fighting.

One form of entertainment was created in 1634 in the little Bavarian village of Oberammergau. A man returning to Oberammergau for Christmas was carrying the bubonic plague. He died from the plague, and the sickness began to spread in the little town. Several inhabitants made a vow that if they were spared, they would perform a passion play every ten years. After the vow was made, not another inhabitant of the town died from the bubonic plague, and all of the town members still suffering from the plague recovered.

The town started the tradition of performing a play depicting the passion and resurrection of Jesus Christ using only town inhabitants as actors and support staff.[107] It is performed every 10 years (2000, 2010, etc.) with half of the town residents taking part and people flocking from all over the world to see the performance.

The 1600s hosted a rich variety of theatrical productions across Europe. Shakespeare's plays debuted between 1590 and 1613. This was the time when the open-air Globe Theater was built in London. Shakespeare's plays were exported to Germany, and they were intended for common people who could not read or write. Around 1600 Wolfhart Spangenberg established a theater in Strasbourg and wrote plays for German audiences.[108]

In the 1500s, the clown was introduced to German audiences. He became a buffoon—a stock character called either "Harlequin" or "Hanswurst." He provided coarse humor with his gross antics—all of which delighted the illiterate audiences.[109]

Pieter Brueghel the Elder painted scenes of peasant life, such as this painting, *Children's games*, painted in 1560.

Peasant Dance captures peasants in lively dancing.

The Wedding Dance illustrates how peasants indulged in big celebrations.

In winter, peasants enjoyed the outdoors by ice skating.

There were other new forms of entertainment. Ice skating became popular. Metal ice skates were introduced in the 1400s.[110] Germans had learned to ice skate in the Middle Ages using skates made from sections of animal leg bones. Swimming was especially popular—typically skinny dipping in rivers.

Professional musicians played a growing variety of instruments—lute, guitar, violin, fiddle, recorder, flute and trumpet. We read that in the 1600s, violins were the music of choice in the saloons where men gathered to enjoy the women of easy virtue.[111]

Acrobats, tumblers and jugglers were always in demand as entertainers.[112] There was definitely a dark side to some of the pleasures of this age. We read that drinking and drunkenness increased everywhere in the 1500s.[113] In fact, German engravings from the 1500s and 1600s of peasant activities almost invariably show one of the guests turning around on his bench to throw up his excess of drink.[114] What is remarkable is that despite their poverty and despite the suffering of wars and plagues, the German peasant were hungry for excuses to have a party. Whether the occasion was a wedding, a birthday, a religious holiday or an ancient pagan festival, they loved a good party with music, dancing, good food and plenty of beer and pherhaps a story teller or entertainer.

Finally, there was one completely new source of pleasure introduced after 1450—smoking. When Columbus arrived in the New World in 1492, he noticed natives smoking rolled tobacco leaves. The tobacco plant was cultivated first in Spain in 1558, and tobacco spread quickly through Europe. Tobacco was first taken in pipes, later in cigars and finally in cigarettes beginning in 1708.[115]

Standard of living

In this period, we will look at the standard of living from two aspects. First, what were the broad economic upturns and downturns, and how did they affect German peasants? Second, did the typical standard of living improve or worsen compared to the High and late Middle Ages of 955–1450?

Let's start with the economic upturns and downturns that swept through all of Europe, as well as those that focused on the German lands after 1450. We start with the Spanish reaching the New World and importing tons of precious metals back to Spain. By means of forced labor, the Spanish required the Incas in Peru and the Aztecs in Mexico to mine gold and silver. The figures are astonishing. Between 1521 and 1650, the official reports of Spain recorded importing two hundred tons of gold and eighteen thousand tons of silver.[116] This was an unimaginable increase in wealth for the Spaniards. When there is more wealth chasing a stable supply of goods and services, the effect is a sharp increase in prices—rampant inflation. Because Spain traded with other European countries, there was a broad trend of inflation between 1521 and 1650. For example, in 1650, wheat prices in western and central Europe (including the German lands) were four times what they had averaged a hundred years before. There was a tendency for wages to lag behind. This combination of persistent increases in prices with only slowly increasing wages caused much distress in individuals.

This inflation from 1521 to 1650 affected all of Europe, but the German lands also suffered their own economic troubles. The opening of trade routes to India, as well as the new trade with the Americas, caused the two major trade networks of the German lands to decline in importance: both the Hanseatic League ports near the Baltic as well as the overland trade routes that enriched cities such as Nuremberg and Augsburg.[117] It happened rather quickly—between 1475 and 1525. At this very time, feudalism was changing toward the formation of a property-less, wage-laboring class. Increasingly, the rural peasants were transformed from paying for leased land with their sweat labor to becoming landless paupers forced into uncertain lives of day labor.

This combination of woes hurt the German lands. It was a time when the economy of England was expanding, and the German economy grew less rapidly or stagnated.[118] After 1550, the German population expansion came to an end. On a relative basis, the German people lagged behind other Europeans in terms of economic well-being from 1475 to the late 1500s.

We see this German lag in the research of Robert C. Allen, an Oxford University economist, who devised a ratio of average wages and compared it to a basket of consumer goods needed for survival in Europe, covering various fifty-year periods from 1500 to 1900. He first charts the nominal wages (expressed in grams of silver) for a laborer in different parts of Europe beginning in 1500–1549.

Average Wages of a Laborer			
	1500–1549	1600–1649	1700–1749
Non-German average	2.8	5.7	5.1
German average	2.9	3.9	3.6

We quickly see that after being on a par with the rest of Europe between 1500 and 1549, the workers' nominal pay lagged significantly behind the rest of Europe over the next two hundred years. If we use the typical pay for day laborers as a proxy for the approximate income of a peasant farmer, we see that incomes in the German lands lagged behind France, Italy, Belgium and England.

But what about prices? If wages lagged behind, perhaps prices also lagged behind, and this would offset any disadvantage to the German people. Let us turn again to the meticulous research of Robert Allen. He compiled a basket of goods for food, fuels and other necessities to sustain a subsistence life in those periods and compiled a price index. The higher the index, the higher the cost of this same basket of goods.

Average Consumer Price Index for Subsistence Living			
	1500–1549	1600–1649	1700–1749
Non-German avg.	5.2	1.21	0.96
German avg.	5.3	1.33	1.02

The price index figures are surprising. Despite the lower German wages, prices of necessary goods are actually a little higher in the German lands than in the other European areas.

What we really want to identify is the "livability index." For this, we divide the cost of the consumer goods into the typical wages. If the result is 1.0, the wages exactly cover the cost of living. If the result is more than 1.0, the worker enjoys a surplus of income. A ratio of less than 1.0 means that the worker cannot afford the basics of life. Economist Robert Allen calls this his "Welfare Ratio."

The "Welfare Ratio"			
	1500–1549	1600–1649	1700–1749
Non-German avg.	1.15	0.98	1.0
German avg.	1.10	0.63	0.70

In the Welfare Ratio table above, we see that the people in the German lands enjoyed a slim surplus from 1500 to 1549, but then the bottom fell out. Over the ensuing two hundred years, Germany suffered through a miserable combination of high prices and low wages resulting in abysmal welfare ratio scores.[119] While the "welfare ratio" is abstract, the grim faces of a peasant family painted in 1640 give graphic expression to their apathy of the typical German pauper.

Why did Germany fall behind? Beginning in 1590, all of Europe faced a series of economic troubles. The 1590s was a decade of recession, followed by a general downturn in the European economy that lasted until about 1620. Throughout this period, there was rampant inflation.[120] People resorted to shaving the edges of the silver penny coins. By shaving small bits of silver and collecting them, they could create a small stash of these shavings that they could take to a silversmith and convert into cash. Silver pennies were the most valuable coin most peasants ever touched. Shaving the coins was illegal, of course, but it was called "Kippen." A specific number of silver pennies were supposed to weigh a pound at this time. Soon merchants were weighing the pennies rather than simply counting them.

The abysmal "Welfare Index" in the German lands is reflected in the faces of this family.

Then in the early 1600s, when the European economy pulled out of its downturn, the German lands were locked into the devastation of the Thirty Years' War. By the war's end in 1648, much of the German territory had been ravaged, and some historians believe it took Germany until about 1750 to return to the economic level of 1618.[121] Of course, the economic devastation of the war was uneven. For example, Hamburg was spared the destruction, but in general urban life in 1675 was less prosperous than it had been in 1575. Germany was becoming an economic backwater because the center of European trade had moved westwards to the Atlantic, and many German towns were no longer the flourishing centers of trade and that they had been in the earlier 1500s.[122]

In summary, the economic conditions of Europe had ups and downs between 1450 and 1650, but the German lands had some unique troubles in that period so that by 1650 the typical German had a lower standard of living than most other Europeans. The German lands probably had more than their share of the outcasts—prostitutes and cripples, paupers and beggars as seen in the illustration.

Whether the typical German peasant was poorer or less poor in 1650 than they were in 1450 is hard to estimate. One source gives a grim picture of the dour circumstances of people in 1475, reporting, "Most Europeans went to sleep hungry most of the time, and most of them were sick. . . . An unbalanced diet low in iodine led to goiter . . . lack of vitamin-rich vegetables during much of the year led to bad teeth and crooked legs (rickets) . . . a diet low in protein resulted in weak bones and muscles."[123]

There were more prostitutes and cripples, paupers and beggars.

A sense of time and place

This period began to shake the foundations of peasants' perspective of time and place. In terms of time, the calendar changed in 1582. In fact, ten days were skipped altogether. This change must have raised many questions.[124] Peasants were becoming aware of the calendar years. They were becoming aware of their age. They must have noticed that changes were still evolving but evolving a little faster than in the Middle Ages.

In 1450 virtually everyone believed that the sun revolved around the earth, but Copernicus challenged that long-held assumption in 1543. It must have been a long time before the notion of a helio-centric universe percolated down to the consciousness of peasants, but gradually it did. Of course, this raised more questions. Do the other planets also revolve around the sun? What about our moon? And all those stars in the sky— where are they located?

For the devout Roman Catholics of this era, the cosmology was quite clear. We are born on this earth to live a short and difficult life. But the whole point of that life is to achieve eternal life in heaven when we die. The difficulties of our lives are only temporary difficulties and are of little significance in the great scheme of things when we think about enjoying eternity in heaven. Hell was feared and dreaded.

The age of exploration was filled with startling new discoveries. The Portuguese discovered the location of the Spice Islands. Then Columbus discovered previously unknown lands across the ocean. This discovery was so dramatic that people began calling it the "new world." Then in 1519, Magellan took five ships on a voyage around the world. Although Magellan was killed and four of the five ships did not make it, one ship successfully sailed all around the world.

These voyages brought back wonderful discoveries—from tobacco that you could smoke to new foods and new drinks (tea and coffee and hot chocolate). This began to change the world view of an illiterate peasant. For a young girl in this time period, "her main source of news would have been what she was told in church or what her father heard in the pub, perhaps from a foreign visitor. She would have been expected to lead the same kind of life that her mother lived, in the same place, and nothing else would have seemed possible to her."[125] But now that was beginning to change.

Part Two:
1650–1850
The Recent Period

Major historical events

I have chosen three major historical events for this period.

1789: French Revolution
1848: The year of revolutions
1871: Unification of the German lands into Germany

The French Revolution exploded in 1789 with the confiscation of the powers of the king, the nobility and the Roman Catholic Church. Those changes served as models of hope for many German peasants. However, the liberation of France was soon transformed into the oppression from Napoleon and imperial France.

When Napoleon's armies invaded and occupied Germany, they brought certain instruments of a new world order—the Napoleonic Code established individual civil rights and voting rights. This code also supported the principles of meritocracy for the positions in the government and for promotion in the army. There were many German peasants who preferred to be ruled by an invading foreign power than to continue to be harassed by their local landlord. Most of the German lands were occupied by the French from 1804 to 1813. And even though the enlightened ideas of Napoleon created somewhat improved living conditions for German peasants, being occupied by the Napoleonic armies meant being subjugated by their historical enemy, the French. Napoleon's defeat at Waterloo in 1815 marked the final end of this French threat.

1848 was the year of revolutions. It started in France in 1846 with a financial crisis and a bad harvest, followed the next year by an economic depression. One report said that there were more than one hundred and thirty thousand abandoned children in France. In early 1848 France outlawed political gatherings, and that sparked the revolt. Crowds flooded the streets of Paris on February 22. In one gathering, a soldier fired his musket. He was joined by his fellow soldiers shooting into the crowd. Fifty-two people were killed, and Paris erupted. Thousands took to the streets, set up barricades to obstruct the army, and began marching on the royal palace. King Louis Philippe quickly abdicated and fled to England.

Armed protest at Alexanderplatz.

Word of these events spread to Germany and other countries. Spontaneous demonstrations exploded across Germany, including Berlin, where people threw up barricades in the streets at Alexanderplatz. In Berlin, the Prussian king, Frederick William IV, was protected by thousands of Prussian troops, but he feared for his safety. He rode through the city wearing the revolutionary colors of Germany.

Across the German lands, delegates were sent to Frankfurt am Main for a parliament that began meeting on May 18 at the large Paulskirche (church) in downtown Frankfurt am Main. They began to debate. Their assumption was that the revolution was already successful, and they were meeting to work out the details of the new political system. There were several hundred delegates. Most of them were well-educated liberals—teachers and lawyers, middle-level government officials, judges, professors, doctors, writers, Catholic priests and Protestant pastors. They represented the professional class. There was not a single working man and only one peasant in the entire assembly.[126] They spent weeks and months debating, reading papers and voting on resolutions. They talked about universal suffrage, trial by jury, the election of army officers and other reforms to the system.

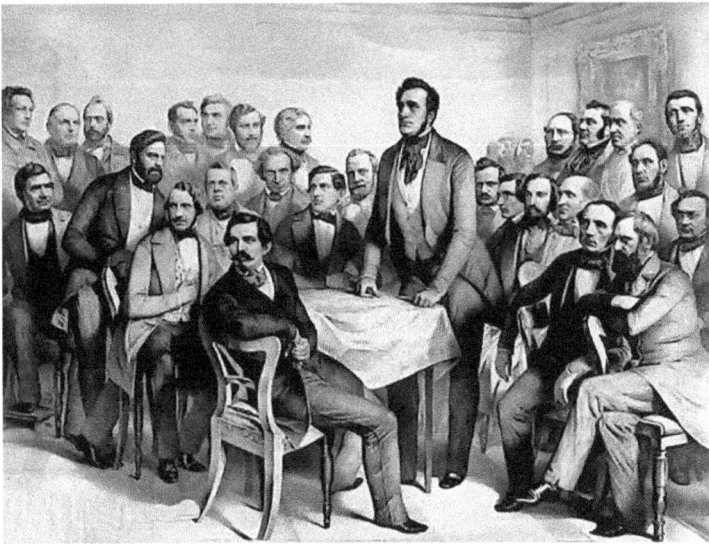

The parliament delegates discussed and debated for eleven months.

They continued their deliberations for months. They had total confidence that all of Germany would unite shortly under the new arrangements they were devising. It is important to note that these men believed in the power of persuasion. They were not motivated by class interest. They were offended by disorder and revolution. Nothing good would come of the intrusion of the masses into politics.[127]

After eleven months of deliberation, the parliament decided to offer the Imperial Crown to Frederick William IV. By this time, he had regained his nerve. He was also reassured by his generals that his Prussian army was eager to put down this rebellion. He rejected the crown saying he would not "pick up a crown from the gutter."[128]

Now the parliament was at a standstill. The more moderate members in Frankfurt simply went home. The more radical decided to return to the barricades and fight. They were soon defeated, and the leaders were executed. A number fled for their lives, emigrating to America. It was all over. As the author A. J. P. Taylor acidly describes it, "At this turning point, Germany did not turn."

In hindsight, we can see what they did wrong:

1. They should have used force to occupy the main government buildings as quickly as possible.
2. They should have solicited desertions from the Imperial Army and gathered volunteers to fight the Imperial Army if necessary.
3. They should have set up a provisional government to keep things running while they worked out their reforms.
4. They should have recruited working people and peasants to their assembly, and with their input, they should have prepared a reform program that addressed the grievances and needs of the working class and the peasants.

The unification of Germany in 1871 was accomplished with Prussian military power and Prussian strategy. In 1640 the province of Prussia was a small, rural province with holdings scattered across northern Germany, but it had a strong king, Friedrich William, the Great Elector. He reigned from 1640 to 1688, and he first put Prussia on the map. Because Prussia was rural and poor and had a small population, the country offered incentives for German farmers to migrate to Prussia. Prussia established an early policy of running an efficient government and a strong army. In 1862 during the reign of King William I, Otto von Bismarck became the chief minister of Germany. He operated on a "Prussia first" policy. He further strengthened the army, and he won the support of the Prussian nobility by reserving virtually all the key officer positions for men of noble birth.

German soldiers march at the Arc de Triomphe in 1871.

In the years leading up to German unification in 1871, Prussia first engineered a small war with Denmark over Schleswig-Holstein, which Prussia won easily in 1864.[129] Then, in 1866, Prussia picked a fight with the Austrian Habsburg Empire. It is safe to say that when the war broke out, most of the German kingdoms sympathized with the Austrians, who had a much larger population and larger army. To the surprise of most, the war was over in three weeks, with Austria suffering a decisive defeat on July 3, 1866, in Koeniggraetz. Prussia used the new railroads and good military tactics to defeat the larger adversary.[130] Now Bismarck was ready for the big challenge—a decisive war with France.

Prior to this time, Germany had been divided into dozens of small defenseless kingdoms, and throughout the 1700s and 1800s, France had easily invaded and defeated various small kingdoms. France had occupied and annexed German territory in Alsace-Lorraine. France had always been the feared bully, but this time it would be different.

War was declared between Germany and France in 1870. This was the key moment. Bismarck persuaded other German kingdoms to join in a united German campaign against the age-old rival. It was the patriotism of joining other German speakers in fighting against a long-time adversary that spurred other German kingdoms to join in the war. Early in 1871, Paris surrendered to the Germans. Within nine years, between 1862 and 1871, Prussia had risen from being the weakest and least regarded of the Great Powers to becoming the dominant state of the European continent. The various German kingdoms, large and small, then agreed in 1871 to join Prussia in a united German nation.[131]

New developments

I have selected eight new developments that impacted peasant lives in Germany between 1650 and the migration years of the 1800s:

1. 1550–1800 Age of Absolutism
2. 1715–1789 Enlightenment (Age of Reason)
3. 1760–1830 Industrial Revolution
4. 1800–1850 Romanticism
5. 1806–1813 French occupation
6. 1813–1871 Birth of German nationalism
7. 1815 Rise of towns and cities in the German lands
8. 1816–1910 Migration out of Germany

First, the "Age of Absolutism" is a label pinned to the period between 1550 and 1800. This era reached its high-water mark during the reign of

Louis XIV in France from 1643 to 1715. He exemplified the unlimited power of his rule as King of France. Throughout Europe, rulers believed in absolutism. No power challenged their unlimited authority. In some cases, these kings claimed to rule by divine right. This notion of "I have absolute authority" seeped into the worldview of many of the hundreds of princes who ruled the German lands. In generation after generation, the princes and landlords of countless regions in the German lands believed that they had every right to do as they pleased. When a group of peasants brought a grievance to the local landlord accusing him and his court of trampling their crops with their hunting party, the prince invariably dismissed their grievances without a thought. Because he had absolute authority and all rights, it followed that they (the grieving peasants) had no authority and no rights.

Second, the Enlightenment is usually dated from 1715 (the year of the death of Louis XIV) and ended in 1789 (the violent French Revolution). Historians have called this period "the Enlightenment" or sometimes "the Age of Reason" because it was a reaction to absolutism. The leaders of the Enlightenment rejected certain principles and promoted other principles. They were against the absolute authority of secular rulers, and they argued for individual rights—"certain inalienable rights," as it was worded in the United States Declaration of Independence. Enlightenment leaders were also opposed to the overreaching authority of the church. They argued for a separation of church and state at a time when many European countries were *de facto* theocracies. They also expressed skepticism about many religious beliefs. They were proponents of reason and the scientific method as a path to truth. The most famous German of the Enlightenment was Immanuel Kant (1724–1804), who said that enlightenment released people from their intellectual bondage. He urged people to "have courage to use your own reason."

Third, the Industrial Revolution is usually bookended to encompass the period of 1760 and 1830 in England. I would trace its progress with the following narrative: England was running out of firewood. The country sought a substitute and began using coal, which was plentiful in England. But they had problems in mining coal when they dug below the groundwater level because water kept filling the mine shafts. They needed pumps to drain the water so they could continue mining. Pumps were invented and then improved using small steam engines. Coal was heavy and expensive to ship, so canals were dug to ship the coal inland. Then trains (with coal-fired steam engines) were established to carry the coal from the mine to a population center or seaport. The profusion of pumps and railroad tracks fueled a need for more iron. Iron railroad tracks were too soft for heavy railroad trains, and this created a need for a stronger type of iron. The need was met by steel and the coke fuel that made the steel. At the same time, the textiles industry was looking for cheaper and faster ways to spin thread and weave thread into cloth. Inventions appeared to meet those needs. The supplies of coal, iron and textiles generated trade, and trade created a need for a workable banking system.

The Industrial Revolution was exported from England to Germany.

Historians debate the Industrial Revolution and its impact on the German lands. They take one of the following two approaches:

1. The original Industrial Revolution never impacted the German lands. Instead, Germany participated in the so-called Second Industrial Revolution, which was triggered in 1870.

2. The Industrial Revolution was imported from England into Germany piece by piece.

I believe the second approach is more accurate because many developments took place before 1870. The first steam engine of English design was installed at a mine near Duisberg in 1753,[132] and the first textile machines were built in Chemnitz in 1782. The first fully steam locomotive powered railway line opened in 1837, linking Leipzig and Dresden with a 117-kilometer standard gauge railroad track.[133]

It is clear that in the late 1700s, German peasants were finding their lives impacted (mostly negatively) by the Industrial Revolution. For example, poor peasant families that earned most of their livelihood by spinning yarn or weaving cloth in their homes were soon put out of business by the faster, new machines in England and elsewhere. It was not until about 1850 that the new sources of power and the efficiencies of machines began to improve the standard of living of German peasants.

Fourth, romanticism is the label given to the artistic spirit in the German lands from 1800 to 1850. Romanticism was a reaction against the cold rationality of the Enlightenment. Romanticism's themes were the healing power of art, the primacy of feeling, the pain of loneliness and the search for community.[134] Romanticism was expressed in music (think Beethoven), painting (Caspar David Friedrich) and literature (E. T. A. Hoffmann and Johann Herder). Romanticism was about the importance of emotion and intuition. It celebrated nature. It glorified the past and sometimes revived medievalism. Of course, the German peasants who lived during the two hundred years beginning with 1650 were largely unaware and indifferent to these labels and untouched by many of the fruits of these periods. They didn't go to college. They never became participants in the arguments about Enlightenment vs. Absolutism vs. Romanticism. It is unlikely they ever heard Beethoven's music, saw a painting by Caspar David Friedrich or read anything written by E. T. A. Hoffmann.

Two men contemplating the moon by Caspar David Friedrich.

Fifth, the French occupation of the German lands lasted from 1806 to 1813. The French occupation brought new values. The nobility was powerless. There was a spirit of meritocracy. The French established a government that rewarded hard work, brains and skill. They promoted universal suffrage. The German peasants must have felt ambivalent. They must have hated being conquered and occupied by their traditional enemy, the French. On the other hand, they must have welcomed the fresh breezes of these French values.

Sixth, the birth of German nationalism took place during the transition years of 1813 to 1871. The dozens of small German kingdoms were defenseless against the united power of France. Being weak, helpless and occupied was a high price to pay for the independence of each little kingdom. Other countries were united—France, England, Spain, Russia. The seeds of patriotism and nationalism were planted in most Germans in the years between 1813 and 1871. They spoke the same language. They had similar customs. They shared the same history. All of this combined to feed a longing in many Germans to have their own country—a united Germany.

This mural was painted on the wall of the Paulskirche for the meeting of the parliament there in 1848. It became the symbol of German patriotism and nationalism.

Seventh, through all the changes in the German lands, "the population in 1800 was heavily rural with only 10 percent of the people living in communities of 5,000 or more and only 2 percent living in cities of more than 100,000. After 1815 the urban population grew rapidly, due primarily to the influx of young people from the rural areas. Berlin grew from 172,000 in 1800 to 826,000 in 1870."[135]

This new development brought other changes:

1. Fewer people worked as subsistence farmers, and more were working at making things, trading, working as merchants, or carters.

2. Those who worked in towns and cities had more opportunities to improve their standard of living.
3. The city dwellers were also exposed to new experiences and became more accepting of change. These were the people who implemented the industrial revolution in the German lands.

A German crowd boarding an emigration ship.

Eighth, emigration to America began when a small group of Mennonites left Germany in 1683 and came to the United States in search of religious freedom. But the first significant wave was in 1816, after a disastrous harvest. Emigration did not have a single cause. The main reasons for emigrating were religious freedom, freedom from the draft and economic opportunity.[136]

When transportation improved and popular knowledge about the new world increased, economic and social pressures led more and more people to consider pulling up their roots and leaving Europe. A typical emigrant was someone from the middle strata, a man with a little property and some skills, who usually traveled with his family. Very few wealthy nobles left their lives of privilege, and those who were paupers had neither the money nor the imagination to start life anew in a land far away.

After this gush of emigrants in 1816, more and more Germans knew someone who had emigrated to the United States, and most of those in America were sending back reports of their good experiences. These letters from the United States were important because the letters painted a picture of freedom from oppression and unimagined economic opportunities.

How they lived

Most aspects of the way peasants lived changed little from the previous period. Many houses were still small one-room affairs. They lacked running water, so the house had no "bathroom." Houses also remained quite dark, although this period brought more lighting in the form of oil lamps. Of course, oil lamps had been common since biblical times. They were ceramic dishes with a wick, and they burned any flammable oil such as olive oil. Olive oil lamps never became common in German lands because of the lack of olive trees in Germany. Therefore, candles remained the principal source of light for hundreds of years. However, candles remained expensive. The cheap candles continued to burn smelly beef tallow. The beeswax candles continued to be too expensive for a typical German peasant. One paid dearly for this "victory over the night."

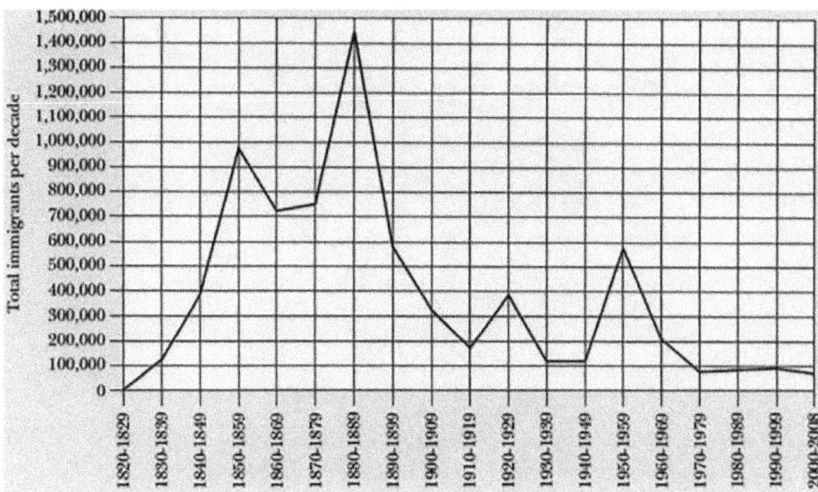

German immigration peaked between 1850 and 1890.[137]

German immigration to the United States	
Immigration Period	Number of Immigrants
1820–1840	160,335
1841–1850	434,626
1851–1860	951,667
1861–1870	787,468
1871–1880	718,182
1881–1890	1,452,970
1891–1900	505,152
1901–1910	341,498

Beginning in the 1700s, whale oil became available. Whale oil was making fortunes for the fishermen of Holland and Hamburg.[138] Whale oil was expensive, but these lamps burned brighter and more evenly than candles and threw back the darkness considerably better.[139]

Whale oil lamps were an improvement over candles.

We will see that changes in housing continued to be slow and sporadic. The fact is that not all housing changed. Indeed, the poorest, most primitive one-room huts continued in existence with little change all the way to 1850. But as the peasantry became more diversified, we see the more prosperous and innovative peasants making improvements to their living quarters—cast iron stoves, better chimney, coal replacing wood as fuel for fires, more glass windows, multiple rooms and oil lamps replacing candlelight. Let's look at housing in this period.

Around 1720, there were changes in the technology of chimneys. The secrets of the "draft" were discovered. The hearth of the chimney was made narrower and deepened. The mantle was lowered, and the chimney shaft was curved because the straight chimney showed a persistent tendency to smoke.[140] It was the beginning of a revolution in home heating which soon brought the stove.

Although this iron stove was actually in use in the period before 1850, this shows how the stove was used for cooking as well as heating.

The legend tells us that Benjamin Franklin invented the Franklin stove as early as 1741, but it did not appear in peasant homes until the early 1800s. The appearance of the cookstove was dependent on improvements in the technology of cast iron. The stove was a major improvement in housing because it not only served to heat the house, it also served as a cookstove. As a cookstove, it had two advantages over the open fire in a fireplace. First, it enclosed the flame, which greatly reduced the danger of the cook or children getting burned or the house catching fire. Second, it allowed the cook to work at waist height instead of bending down to the floor. Third, the early stoves were made of iron, vented through a metal pipe that funneled the smoke outside. Smoke was virtually eliminated in the house.[141]

Stoves immediately saved firewood because the stove could limit the amount of air feeding the flame and thus reduce fuel consumption. The very first stoves burned firewood, but stoves were introduced in the German lands just as coal was replacing firewood in much of the world, and soon stoves were burning coal. The stove was placed in the center of the room, and it radiated heat in all directions to warm the house—or at least the area around the stove.

There was some resistance to these new stoves. Many peasants preferred the open fire because they liked the cheerful open flames. On the coldest days of winter, it was very difficult to heat the house adequately. In fact, during the "Little Ice Age" of the 1690s, approximately 10 percent of the population of Scandinavia died. Poor people were in danger of freezing to death in their own homes.[142] This was a period of transition from firewood to coal. By 1603 coal had become the primary fuel used in English homes, and coal quickly spread to other European countries. There were times when peasants spent as much as 10 percent of their income on coal.[143]

Coal stoves were high-maintenance appliances. They required much more time and attention than an open wooden fire. The first problem was getting the coal to burn. Greasy paper might be put into the fire box along with wood shavings, and then larger strips of wood crisscrossed to allow airflow but to keep the coal from falling through. A little coal could then be added, but not too much. An updraft in the chimney pipe might need to be started by thrusting a burning wisp of paper into it. Ashes had to be periodically shaken loose and more coal added. The dampers and vents also had to be continually adjusted to control air flow and speed of combustion. Stoves were often kept burning all day and sometimes all night. This offered three benefits: It eliminated the bother of rekindling. It kept a reservoir of warm water ready for washing, and it radiated heat into the house. Of course, there was also the daily task of carrying in the coal—about 50 pounds each day—and carrying out the cinders.[144]

Another improvement during this time was windows. Plate glass for windows could only be produced by casting. There were key breakthroughs in this casting technology from 1650 to 1700. This made it possible for Versailles and its Hall of Mirrors to be constructed in the late 1600s. It was the Venetians who perfected the new technique. As much as two thousand pounds of glass were introduced by stages into a huge crucible. This molten glass was heated with a coal fire to disperse the bubbles and then poured out on the casting table that had movable guides to determine the size of the sheet. While still molten, a state in which it remained for scarcely a minute, the glass was rolled to produce a sheet with an even surface and uniform thickness.[145]

Mirrors had become important, not only for Versailles but for surveying and navigation—not to mention domestic washing and grooming.

Windows remained relatively small and few in number. They usually were covered with paper or other materials such as waxed linen.[146] However, the technology of casting plate glass had improved markedly, especially with the use of coal in firing the glass. This pushed the cost of plate glass down, and it was now affordable for almost everyone. Hence, even peasants could usually afford several glass windows. Panes of window glass continued to increase in size and decrease in cost from the 1600s going forward.[147] This meant more light in the house.

Many new houses were built with timber framing. The timbers were heavy wooden posts and beams held together with interlocking joints using a protruding tenon to fit into a carefully cut mortise. The spaces between the wood frameworks were filled with wattle and daub or other locally available materials, including stone or brick. The chinks between the log walls were nearly always filled with mud and clay and even manure, and in winter, the house was banked around with branches to keep out the cold.[148]

The "balloon framing" technique, where the framework was built of many lightweight 2 x 4s, was not invented until the 1830s in Chicago. This would be a major breakthrough because it used smaller dimension boards, and they could be nailed together. But this revolutionary building technique did not reach Germany until well after 1850.

Change was slow, and the countryside remained filled with the traditional wattle and daub houses. Since the Iron Age, this had been the typical building technique of mixing clay with straw and pressing it into a mixture of reeds and willow twigs. These flimsy houses were still found in Germany through 1850. In fact, when John Quincy Adams was serving as the ambassador to Prussia in 1800, he traveled from Berlin to Frankfurt an der Oder and was surprised to find houses "meager compositions of mud and thatch in which a ragged and pallid race of beggars reside."[149] As late as 1906, a survey in Romania found that 31 percent of the rural homes were made of wattle and daub.

What had changed by 1650 was that the peasant class had become much more diverse. There were now rich peasants who had enough money to buy out the estate of a nobleman who went bankrupt. These well-to-do peasants built comfortable houses for themselves of stone and brick and sometimes with elaborate decorations and expensive furnishings. They were also able to buy solid, comfortable furniture, including chairs, which now featured backs and arms.[150]

We are fortunate to have a vivid description of one community of wealthy peasants in 1684—the village of Leimbach, located between Frankfurt am Main and Kassel. There were six peasant farms ranging in size from 74 acres to 106 acres. These families practiced impartible inheritance in which the entire farm was deeded to the oldest surviving son. Each farmhouse was located on a square facing an inner courtyard. Each of the six farms had multiple buildings. The family lived in the "young" house facing the street. There was an "elders" house set off by itself where the elderly owner retired when he turned the farm over to his oldest child. But well-to-do peasants were very much the exception.

Most peasants continued to live in huts that were small, uncomfortable and unhealthy. Many had only one room or one room used as living quarters and a second room that served for storage or as a stable. Not infrequently, the floor was dirt. The hut held a few pieces of crude furniture that included a table, benches along the wall, a shelf or two and perhaps a cupboard. There was usually a cast-iron pot, a cauldron, a basin, a pail, some barrels, tubs, wooden or earthenware plates, an ax, a spade and a knife. Frequently there was no chimney, and the walls were blackened by smoke that could escape through a hole poked in the roof. The small windows let in very little light, so the hut's interior was dark, damp and gloomy. Lighting often was provided by burning pine stocks.[151]

Many peasants continued to share their one- or two-room huts with their animals. Pigs, ducks, chickens and calves lived together with their owners. Large animals usually were in nearby sheds or lean-tos. One can imagine the stench inside that house after a night in which all the windows were closed.[152]

Typical sights, sounds and smells

A sight that would be startling to our eyes was the semi-public use of chamber pots for relieving oneself. We have learned that privacy was a very rare commodity at this time. There were no private bathrooms. Men, women and children simply relieved themselves into the ever-present chamber pots. In fact, one guest was shocked to report that in 1784 he was a dinner guest in a dining room of a European castle. At the conclusion of the meal, the ladies departed for the sitting room, and the men lingered around the table to finish their drinks and enjoy male talk. The host opened a cupboard door to reveal the chamber pot, and several of the guests promptly used it to relieve themselves.[153]

These are examples of early chamber pots.

The first steam-powered trains appeared in the German lands in 1837. This was a dramatic new experience of speed, power and noise. Germans viewed the railroad with fascination. They recorded the first time they saw a locomotive, smoke billowing from its engine, moving through the landscape; they noted the sensations of excitement and anxiety that their first train trip aroused.[154] If a person stood by a railroad track, they would also hear the distinctive whine of the train as it approached. The tone was a higher note, and that note immediately dropped a bit as the train passed and now moved away.

What were the smells of the period? We might think that the smell of manure piles was a thing of the past, but it was even more predominant after 1650 because front door manure piles had become a status symbol. A friend of the author grew up in a small village near Frankfurt during the 1940s, and she reported that as a child, the key status symbol in her village had not changed in several hundred years: who had the tallest dung heap piled at their front door? In cold weather, the dung heap froze, and the smell vanished, but in the heat of summer, it must have been quite potent. Furthermore, as anyone who has spent time on a farm is aware, there are wide variations in the odor of manure ranging from the benign smell of horse droppings to the nasty stench of hog manure.

There were some new smells between 1650 and 1850. One was the smell of burning lamp oil. Oil lamps had become more common, and they began to replace candles as a source of light inside the home. Another smell was the smell of coal smoke. It is not a pleasant smell, but coal was replacing wood as the fuel of choice. When burned indoors, the coal smoke could be smelly and dirty. Another new smell was that of pipe and cigar smoke. Both pipe and cigar smoking had become popular by 1800 in Germany. They were fairly expensive indulgences, so it is unlikely that peasants indulged, but they could have been exposed to secondhand smoke in public places. A good smell also emerged in this era. It was the smell of freshly brewed coffee. Coffee became a popular home beverage in Germany in the early 1800s. We can imagine that there were husbands in those days who arose early to start the pot of coffee, so their wives awoke to the pleasant aroma.

A piano in Europe in the 1800s.

During this time, Hamburg and the other prosperous cities began to pave the city streets with cobblestones. The "clack-clack" of horse hooves hitting those cobblestone streets was a new sound.

Finally, there was a completely new sound produced by a new instrument called the "piano." The piano had its first blush of popularity when Johann Sebastian Bach gave a piano concert in 1768. By 1800 wealthy Germans were buying pianos for their homes. Imagine yourself as a young child walking down the street past a beautiful home and hearing live piano music for the first time in your life. It must have been mesmerizing.

Work

Crop yields of only three or four to one (or three of four times the seed planted) prevailed, meaning that next year's sowing could take as much as a quarter or one-third of the annual harvest.[155] To stay alive in years of poor harvest, many peasants had to seek out other sources of income, such as day labor or cottage industry. And they borrowed. Their lords advanced them cash, produce or seed. They also borrowed from fellow peasants, who often charged usurious rates of interest. The yields per acre remained little changed since the Iron Age. This was the basic problem for the peasant farmers in 1800. Today in the United States, by comparison, the typical wheat plant has five heads, and each head holds 22 seeds for a total of 110 seeds resulting from a single planted seed. In terms of yields, the typical wheat farmer in the United States sows about 1.8 bushels of seed wheat on each acre and expects to harvest about 100 bushels of wheat per acre, so the ratio of harvest to seed is 55 to 1.

Why was there so little progress in productivity? There are several reasons:

1. The peasants themselves were struggling to survive. They were afraid to try something new and untested.
2. There were always powerful counter-pressures from their social superiors and neighbors to conform and follow.
3. Finally, the lords who owned the land and had the luxury to try new techniques were usually not interested. They were

not motivated to increase production. They were motivated to entertain and show their wealth through conspicuous consumption.

One of the few agricultural breakthroughs of this period was the seed drill invented in England in 1733 by Jethro Tull. This was a farm implement pulled by a draft animal. It had a wheel that rotated, poking a hole in the earth at regular intervals, depositing a seed at a predetermined depth and then covering the seed with soil. The result was that wheat or other grain was now planted in orderly rows. This saved seed, and it facilitated harrowing and harvesting. By 1850 the seed drill had spread to the German lands.

Another agricultural improvement was the increased use of the long-handled scythe over the short-handled sickle. It worked four times faster than the sickle, and by 1850 the scythe had replaced the sickle.

Still another improvement of this period was the move toward the four-crop rotation system. It was devised in England in the 1700s and called the "Norfolk" rotation system. It called for rotating from:

1. Wheat
2. Turnips
3. Barley
4. Clover

In this system, no field is left completely fallow, but the clover crop serves as a "green fallow." Because each family of plants has certain typical insects and diseases associated with it, this constant change served to resist these insects and diseases. Clover was the "king of the green fallow" because it was rich in nutritive matter, gathering nitrogen from the air and spreading it deep into the soil.[156]

A major improvement was the use of fertilizer. Between 1843 and 1854, there was a massive infusion of "guano" (seagull dung) imported from Chile.[157]

The status of a peasant continued to be coded to express the size of that peasant's holding—whether he owned or leased it. The labels had changed slightly. A "full holding" (or *Hufe* in German) varied depending upon the area of the German lands. In Brandenburg, between 1650 and 1850, a *Hufe* comprised 19 acres, but in Saxony, a *Hufe* was anything between 32 and 41 acres. In some areas, a *Hufe* totaled as much as 126 acres. A peasant with a full holding was always considered well-to-do.[158]

Compared to England, France, Italy and the Netherlands, the German lands remained overwhelmingly rural. As late as 1852, fully 71 percent of the Prussian population lived in the countryside.[159] Germany was late to have any large cities. In fact, in 1783, the population of Berlin was 141,000 while the population of London was over 800,000.[160]

A peasant with a full holding and owned a team of draft animals (either oxen or horses) was now known as a *Bauer*. The exact number of draft animals required varied from region to region. A peasant who owned some draft animals but less than the requisite number was called a *Halbbauer*—a "half farmer." This half farmer would seek out another half farmer to put together a full team of draft animals at plowing time. Of course, there were peasants with no draft animals. The man who had no draft animals was a day laborer and was called a *Tauner* or a *Cotter* (cottager). This indicated that the individual lived in a cottage and might have a small garden, but he had no land to grow crops. There was a definite pecking order established for peasants after 1650. This pecking order reflected the evolution of peasants over the centuries in which a few peasant families prospered and became well-to-do while most slipped in their social status as population pressures caused holdings to decrease in size. This decrease is seen in the historical records. In 1550 in Saxony, 50 percent of the peasants had full holdings. In 1750, only 25 percent had full holdings, and in 1843 it was only 14 percent.

A "full holding" (or *Hufe* in German) declined because a peasant who died without any eligible heirs (direct descendants) had no right to sell his land or bequeath it to a brother or nephew. The land reverted to the lord of the manor. The size of holdings also decreased in those areas of the German lands that practiced "partible inheritance," meaning that the father divided up his land, leaving equal parts to each of his children. Since this was a recipe for future poverty, the custom in 80 percent of the German lands had become "impartible inheritance," with the entire holding left to one person.

The growing number of peasants who lacked a full holding meant that they could not support their families by farming a small plot of land. They were forced to seek outside employment. At this time, new opportunities for part-time employment became available such as home spinning or weaving, working in a mine or as a lumberjack or even traveling with a pack of small wares as a peddler. Of course, the changing economy created new kinds of jobs—working as a schoolteacher, working on barges on the newly excavated canals, working on the new railroads.

In 1820 William Jacob reported, "I was in Frankfurt on market day and observed there how much it was crowded with peasants offering their commodities for sale in very small quantities. Some had a few apples, plums, pears or grapes, the whole value of which could not be more than three or fourpence."[161]

A rat catcher illustrates his services for those who cannot read.

Blacksmiths were prominent in every town.

In Saxony, the number of peasants involved in non-farm work (spinners, weavers, miners and other industrial work) increased from 18 percent of the rural population in 1550 to 52 percent in 1843. Spinning and weaving held undisputed first place among rural industries. Both could be done at odd times during the entire year, and all members of the family could participate in the manufacturing process.[162] Wool was the usual raw material, but linen, made from flax that was grown and prepared by the peasant himself, was in many places the principal textile in the region. Because of the prominent role of horses, blacksmiths were in great demand in every city, town and village. We can imagine that the blacksmith shop was a typical gathering place for locals to share news and exchange opinions.

While farmers in 2019 are acutely aware of good breeding techniques to preserve the quality of their livestock, this was very seldom practiced between 1650 and 1850. The general practice was to herd all of the village livestock together, resulting in indiscriminate breeding. In most places, care of the village cattle was entrusted to a herdsman who was paid by the village community. Each morning at the sound of the herdsman's horn, the villagers led their cattle into the village, and the herdsman drove them to the place then in use as pasture. Whether it was a cow or horse, pig or sheep, the breed remained mixed and small in size.[163] In 1800 in the German lands, the size or output of the farm animal contrasted with the figures for recent times.[164]

	In 1800	**Today**
Average cow size	200 kilos	500 kilos
Milk produced per year	1,000 liters	3,700 liters
Pig size	50 kilos	103 kilos
Sheep size	15 kilos	24 kilos

The peasants of this era placed little importance on breeding and raising livestock. They were grain farmers. It was much more efficient to use grain for human consumption than to feed it to animals. It takes about 12 pounds of grain to produce one pound of beef on the hoof, 1.3 pounds of grain to produce 1 pound of milk or about 6 pounds of grain to produce one pound of pork on the hoof. As a result, only about 6 percent of the grain was used to feed farm animals in this period.[165]

There was an important exception to this disdain for the careful breeding of livestock. It was sheep. Until the 1700s, almost all sheep were owned by the landlords because they enjoyed the unique privilege of grazing their flocks on the fields of the peasants. In the 1700s, the landlords recognized that the fleece from Spanish sheep was far superior to that of native animals. Not only was the fleece rich and thick, but it also became pure white when scoured. They learned that these Spanish sheep were Merino sheep. In 1748 the first Merino sheep were imported to the Brandenburg farm of a progressive Prussian landlord. In 1765 the Elector of Saxony brought in an entire flock of 92 rams and 128 ewes of Merino sheep. In 1817 Prussia had eight million sheep; only 9 percent were Merinos, but by 1849 there were 16 million sheep in Prussia and 27 percent were Merinos. Merino wool was sold at a 50 percent premium to common wool.[166]

In hindsight, work had changed relatively little in the previous two thousand years. In 1817 the German population remained almost 80 percent rural. The majority of people continued to be subsistence farmers. They worked outside where they worked the land. They plowed. They planted. They harrowed with the help of a couple of draft animals. They hoped that the unpredictable weather would cooperate. They worked only in the daylight sun. Radical changes would revolutionize every aspect of work in the coming two hundred years.

Today less than 10 percent carry on this tradition of farm labor—and the conditions for that 10 percent are much changed. Now they do their fieldwork using large tractors powered by powerful engines. They have GPS devices to keep their rows straight. They sit in comfortable enclosed cabs and listen to the radio as they work.

But the most radical changes have come to those who no longer work as farmers. Many of these people work with machines. Many work in offices supplemented with telephones and computers. They manipulate information.

Sometimes a new technology creates an occupation. Clocks began to be made around 1650 in the Black Forest in Germany, and clockmakers became very skilled craftsmen.

Clocks were first made in the Black Forest around 1650.

What they ate and drank

The period of 1650 to 1850 brought dramatic changes to the eating and drinking habits of the German people in the form of potatoes, tomatoes, sugar, coffee, cookstoves, and forks.

Let's start with potatoes, the most transformative change in diet. Potatoes had been skillfully cultivated in South America by the Inca Indians for two thousand years before Pizarro discovered this miracle food. The Incas developed hundreds of varieties, each suited to a different combination of sun, soil and moisture. The potato was shipped back to Spain, where it was in cultivation as early as 1570.[167] In the 1580s, the potato was introduced to Ireland. By 1600 potatoes were grown on a small scale in Europe, especially in Italy and the Netherlands. Potatoes consistently met a mixed reception. In country after country, enlightened rulers encouraged the consumption of potatoes, but the people refused to try them.[168]

Experts reported that potatoes could be grown in a wide variety of soils and climates. They were hardy and easy to grow. They required minimal labor—no threshing or grinding as with wheat. Potatoes were very filling and nutritious, and they produced more food value (calories) per acre than wheat, rye or any other alternative. But people resisted saying that potatoes were ugly, knobby and misshapen. They were only fit for pigs. Surely God did not intend his children to eat these strange vegetables.

In 1740 after a bad grain harvest, Frederick the Great urged his subjects to grow potatoes. They refused. The following tale may be apocryphal, but the story claims that Frederick the Great then ordered potatoes to be planted in his royal garden and posted guards to "protect" them. However, each night he withdrew the troops. The local peasants decided that if the crop was worth protecting, it was worth stealing. So, they stole these potato plants, transplanted them and began eating potatoes.[169] They weren't bad.

More people tried potatoes and found them bland but not objectionable. Potato consumption began to accelerate in 1765, and in the next thirty-six years, potato production in some parts of the German lands increased twenty-fold.[170] In 1830 a German scientist concluded that one acre of land could produce eleven thousand pounds of potatoes but no more than fifteen hundred pounds of wheat.[171]

Hernán Cortéz discovered tomatoes growing in Montezuma's garden. He carried back tomato seeds to Spain. The first tomatoes consumed in Europe were small (the size of cherry tomatoes) and yellow. Initially, they were suspected of being poisonous, but they became a popular food in Europe between 1780 and 1800.

Sugar first appeared from sugar cane grown in the Caribbean. Because it was initially considered a medicine, sugar could only be purchased in apothecaries.[172] A German chemist did some experiments, and in 1747, he discovered how to extract sugar from a number of different plants. He discovered that beetroots produced the most sugar. In the late 1700s, an acre planted in sugar beets would convert into 1,100 pounds of sugar.[173] Between 1800 and 1850, sugar beets began to be grown, and they became an important source of sugar. Sugar spread through Europe in a haphazard fashion. In 1700 it was still unknown in some corners of Europe.[174]

The drinking of tea or coffee spurred the consumption of sugar because sugar was always added to these hot beverages. The drink had to be piping hot in order to melt and dissolve the sugar. The traditional ceramic cups of the day were shaped like small vertical bowls without handles. Of course, a hot cup would burn one's fingers, so this created a need for handles on cups. The cup handle was born in the 1700s, and soon European companies like Wedgwood and Meissen were making porcelain cups with handles.

Coffee originated in Yemen around 1450 and was exported from its main seaport, Mocha. Coffee reached Cairo by 1510. When coffee appeared in Europe, it began as a luxury drink to be enjoyed in coffee houses. A popular story explains that when the Turks retreated from the siege of Vienna in 1683, they left behind some large bags of coffee beans. An enterprising Polish army officer named Kolschitzky knew about coffee. He gathered up the bags and opened Vienna's first coffee house.[175] In the early 1700s, there was a coffee house known to be in Leipzig. Coffee was expensive. In 1700 a one-pound bag of coffee beans imported from Yemen cost the equivalent of twelve dollars in today's money. This meant only the wealthiest could afford it.[176] In 1735 Johann Sebastian Bach debuted his "Coffee Cantata," satirizing those who opposed coffee drinking as unhealthy.[177] Eventually, prices went down, and coffee and tea became wildly popular in England. Tea consumption grew four-hundred-fold in England between 1693 and 1793, but the Germans never joined the tea craze. They preferred coffee.[178] In 1730 coffee plantations were planted in Brazil and Indonesia. These competitors broke the Yemen monopoly and caused a plunge in coffee prices.[179] Coffee quickly assumed its role as a drink for breakfast. Because coffee used boiling water, it was a safe drink. It was also valued for its pharmacological benefits in boosting stamina and mental sharpness.[180]

Cookstoves were another major change that appeared between 1650 and 1850 to replace the open fire in the fireplace. They virtually eliminated smoke, and they made it possible to fry food over a flat hot surface.

In this period water carriers sold fresh, pure water door to door.

During this time, water made something of a comeback. There were now some reliable sources of sanitary water—private wells and fresh springs. The water carrier became a common sight. He carried two wooden barrels of water and sold it from door to door.

The fork was remarkably late to appear in the German lands. For the better part of two thousand years, German peasants made do with knives and spoons. In the 900s, the table fork with two tines was common in the Middle East. In the 1400s, the fork became commonplace in Italy as an implement to use in eating pasta. Catharine de Medici introduced the fork to France in 1550 when she became the queen of France, but the French people resisted. They thought that one's fingers were better equipped for gathering food.

Most of Europe resisted the fork. Some criticized it as an "unmanly Italian affectation." This utensil slowly evolved from two tines to a curved, three-tine model that was finally accepted in the German lands in about 1750. It made its transition to the standard four tines in the early 1800s.[181] The use of the fork established some rules of etiquette. Eating with the fingers was now considered rude and disrespectful. The fork also contributed to sit-down family dinners, which became an important feature in German culture.

Table talk: Trying out potatoes

Gertraud and Waldo Freie sit down to dinner with their four children. The year is 1765, and they live in a small village in Prussia. This is a special night for Gertraud. She is an excellent cook and has been experimenting with different ways to prepare and eat potatoes. She has learned two things from the other housewives in the village. First, potatoes can be a miracle food—delicious, healthy and filling. Second, it can be very difficult to persuade the man of the family to accept them.

There is widespread prejudice against eating potatoes. The prejudice is not confined to her village. It extends throughout most of the German lands. Potatoes look funny. Some people feed them to their pigs, and thus they are sometimes called "pig food." Some rumors suggest they are poisonous. But ultimately, it is all ignorance. Most people in the village have never tasted potatoes, but they are convinced that they don't like them. In the Freie family, there is an extra dynamic. Her four children (all boys) idolize their father. They imitate him in many ways, and they won't eat anything that their father doesn't eat. So, if she cannot convince her husband to eat potatoes, she won't have any potato eaters in the family.

Gertraud is resourceful and determined. She is also a creative cook. She has an instinct for putting together dishes that look and taste good and has turned her attention to potatoes. She has a neighbor friend who grows potatoes in her kitchen garden. Gertraud could do the same if she had an assurance that her family would eat them.

Her husband is a fine partner, but he does have a stubborn streak. There is no point in trying to convince him against his will. She has to get him to enjoy potatoes. Gertraud made a trade with her neighbor and acquired a few potatoes. She peeled and disposed of the skins, then cut up the potatoes and boiled them. Once they were thoroughly cooked, she mashed them.

Now she applied her cooking wizardry. She added some shavings of onions, some melted butter with some salt and a little pepper. Then she mixed in some milk with these mashed potatoes in her large soup kettle over low heat.

At the supper table, each member of the family was seated at their usual place. The room was now suffused with the fragrance of her rich potato soup.

She served supper beginning with a small helping of cold beet soup to her husband and the four boys and then served herself a bowl of this hot creamy potato soup garnished with a sprig of parsley. Everyone could smell her soup. She carefully spooned it into her mouth, closing her eyes to savor the taste. It was delicious.

Her husband Waldo kept glancing at her soup and finally asked: "What are you eating, Gertraud?"

Gertraud: "Oh, it's just a new recipe for soup."

Waldo: "It smells good."

Gertraud ladles a spoonful of soft butter into her bowl of soup. "It tastes pretty good."

Waldo: "What's in it?"

Gertraud: "Oh, a little this and that. I think it needs just a bit more salt." And she shakes a tiny amount of salt into her soup and continues to eat.

Waldo now impatiently: "Well, can you share a taste with your husband?"

By this time, the four boys have stopped eating and are looking at their mother. She shrugs her shoulders and says: "Well, try this." She ladles a spoonful and passes it to him.

Waldo: "Ummmm. It tastes as good as it smells."

Gertraud fakes surprise and says: "Waldo, are you sure you like it?"

Waldo now dips his own spoon into her bowl of soup, takes another taste and says: "Of course, I like it. It's better than your cold beet soup. Do you have any more of that?"

Gertraud: "Well, I might have a little bit more." She returns with a steaming hot bowl of potato soup for Waldo, which he begins to devour.

Waldo: "What do you call that soup?"

Gertraud: "Well, it is sort of a special creation, so I have named it after the day. I call it my *Montag Suppe*. It's a lot of work to prepare."

Waldo: "Do you suppose you could make some more next week for all of us?"

Gertraud smiling: "I suppose so."

Technology

In the years immediately before the Industrial Revolution, Europe was starved for energy. Germany and all of Europe continued to rely on the traditional sources of energy that had been available for almost two thousand years. Let's look at five sources of energy in 1800. I will list them in descending order of importance.

1. Animal traction. In 1800 there were 14 million horses and 24 million oxen in Europe. If we assign a quarter horsepower to each of these 36 million animals, the result is about nine million horsepower.
2. Burning wood was estimated to generate four to five million horsepower each year.

3. Waterwheels were ubiquitous. One source says there was a waterwheel for every twenty-nine people. This large number of waterwheels produced between 1.5 and three million horsepower.
4. It is estimated that the 50 million workers in Europe generated about 900,000 horsepower.
5. The sails of sailing ships converted the wind into about 230,000 horsepower per year.[182]

This list does not include windmills, riverboats, charcoal or coal, but the obvious point is that of the estimated total horsepower listed above, 80 percent was produced by draught animals and firewood. Europe was starved for energy. When the first steam engine was connected to a flour mill, it did five times the work of a waterwheel.

This time period covers the Industrial Revolution, so it is not surprising that between 1650 and 1850, there were many technological breakthroughs. I will list them in a rough descending order of importance, starting with thirteen major breakthroughs followed by six more modest innovations. The major breakthroughs were:

1. The steam engine
2. Antiseptics
3. Anesthesia
4. Seed drill
5. Pasteurization
6. Spinning jenny
7. Flying shuttle
8. Cotton gin
9. Gas lighting
10. Smallpox vaccination
11. Bicycle
12. Sewing machine
13. Pendulum clocks

Steam engines were developed in England, starting with a steam-powered pump designed to drain water out of mines in 1698. This was followed by a piston-driven steam engine invented by Thomas Newcomen in 1712. Hundreds of Newcomen engines were installed in mines around England in the next one hundred years. In 1763 a Scottish inventor named James Watt was asked to repair one of these engines. He was surprised at its wasteful design. He was able to acquire financial backing, and soon his steam engines were being manufactured not only to drain water from mines but also to power steamships beginning in 1802 and steam locomotives as early as 1829.[183]

The credit for antiseptics goes to the Hungarian doctor Ignaz Semmelweis, who published a book in 1861 on his findings and became regarded as the "father of antiseptics."

William Morton was a twenty-seven-year-old dentist who learned about the anesthetic properties of ether while studying chemistry at Harvard. In 1846 he administered ether and performed a painless tooth extraction for his patient. As news spread, a prominent Boston surgeon arranged for a public demonstration in the operating theater of the Massachusetts General Hospital. Again, ether was administered, and a surgeon painlessly removed a tumor from the neck of a patient. News of this successful demonstration quickly spread around the world. Soon other agents such as chloroform were used for anesthesia. It was anesthesia that opened the possibilities of performing all kinds of surgery.

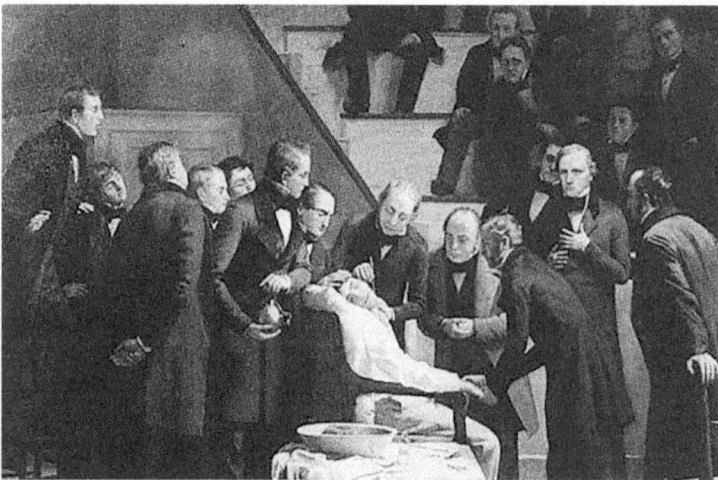

The first successful operation using an anesthetic was in Boston in 1846.

Jethro Tull was an English farmer who invented a "seed drill" in 1701. This sparked a revolution in agriculture. At the time, seed was always cast by hand in a random fashion across the field. This had been the standard practice since year 1. But it had two disadvantages. First, this casting was wasteful of seed. Some areas received too much seed, and some areas too little. Second, this random sowing made it difficult to harrow (chop out the young weeds).

Tull invented a machine that was pulled (like a plow) behind a horse walking in a straight line. The machine carried three boxes of seeds and deposited seeds three rows at a time. Each seed was deposited at the correct depth and correct spacing from each other. This procedure ensured the efficient use of seed grain. But the second benefit was perhaps even more important. Now, the grain was planted in orderly rows. This meant that the farmer could "harrow" the new seedlings by digging out any weed seedlings that sprouted between the rows. Before he died in 1741, he spent the later years of his life improving the seed drill machine and preaching the benefits of harrowing.

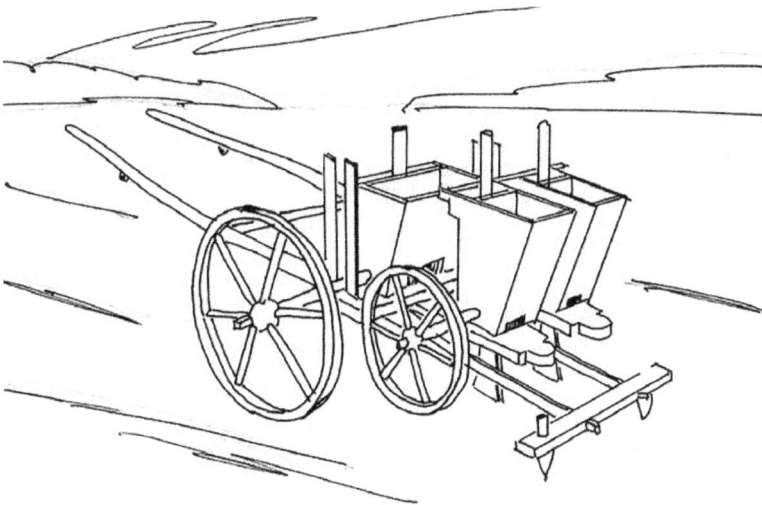

The seed drill was truly revolutionary.

Louis Pasteur is often revered as the father of germ theory. At the time, the leading infection theory was "spontaneous generation."

Between 1850 and 1890, he demonstrated that heating something such as wine or milk could destroy unwanted micro-organisms. His theory was immediately put to use in "pasteurizing" milk to kill off tuberculosis pathogens.

In 1733 the flying shuttle was perfected and patented. It was used to weave yarn or thread into cloth. This machine instantly doubled the productivity of the weaver and quickly doubled the demand for thread.[184]

"Eventually, in about 1765, the spinning jenny was introduced to produce cotton thread at high speeds. The key to its operation was that one large wheel was connected to eight or more spools. The spinner would turn the large wheel by hand, and this made the eight spools rotate, thus spinning the strands into yarn." The spinning jenny geometrically increased the speed of spinning yarn.[185] The spinning jenny became one of the essential machines to usher in the Industrial Revolution in textiles.

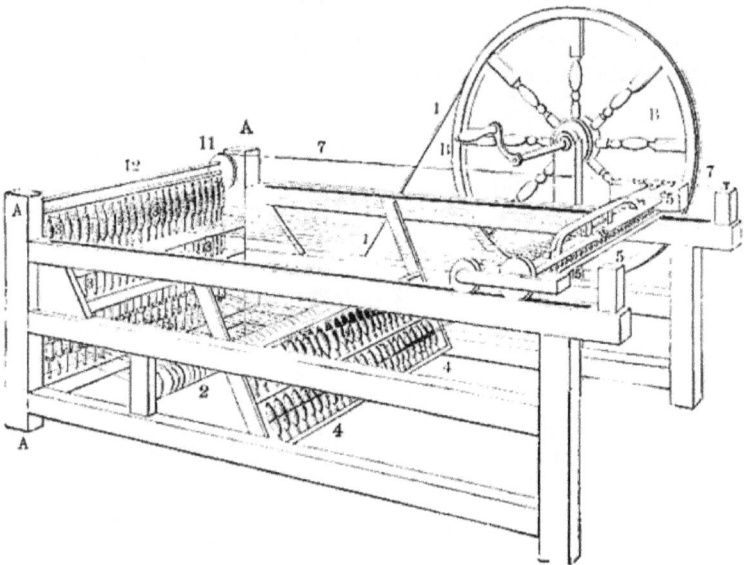

The spinning jenny produced cotton threat at high speeds.

As every American schoolchild learns, the cotton gin was invented by Eli Whitney in 1793. It was designed to replace the hand labor previously required to separate the cotton fibers from their seeds. This machine was a rotating cylinder with small wire hooks and brushes that continuously tore away the seeds from the cotton fibers. It revolutionized the cotton industry by making cotton less labor-intensive and thus much cheaper.

Gas lighting began in about 1800 when companies and cities began to employ a flammable gas (such as coal gas, propane or natural gas) which was distributed through pipes and then lit to provide light for either a factory or for the streets of a city. In 1820 Paris began to light its streets with gas. Gas lighting played a role in the Industrial Revolution because it allowed factory owners to operate their factories for longer hours. The new artificial light would supplement sunlight on shorter winter days.

Dr. Edward Jenner noticed that people who worked with cattle and caught cowpox were not known to catch smallpox. He didn't fully understand the connection, but he theorized that perhaps if someone were inoculated with the mild cowpox, they might be immune to smallpox. He tested his theories in the 1790s and published a paper in 1798. His discovery was not simply protection against smallpox, but it opened up the possibility that other vaccines could be developed to immunize people from specific diseases.

The earliest sewing machines were invented in 1790. A competitive model was introduced in 1804. Elias Howe introduced his sewing machine in 1845, and Isaac Merritt Singer brought out his machine in 1851. Singer eventually won the patent rights. Consumers began purchasing these machines in the 1860s when homemade clothes were still the typical clothing.

The bicycle was an early German invention. In 1817 Baron Karl von Drais invented a two-wheeled vehicle in which the rider rested his butt on a seat, but he didn't sit down and pedal. There were no pedals. Instead, he sat on the bike seat and propelled himself with his feet—like pushing off on a skateboard but alternately with both legs. In 1863 a Frenchman invented the first device that looked and operated something like our modern bicycle with pedals that powered the front wheel. Bicycles became popular in the 1890s and remained the most popular mode of transportation in Europe until about 1950, when more Europeans could afford to buy automobile.

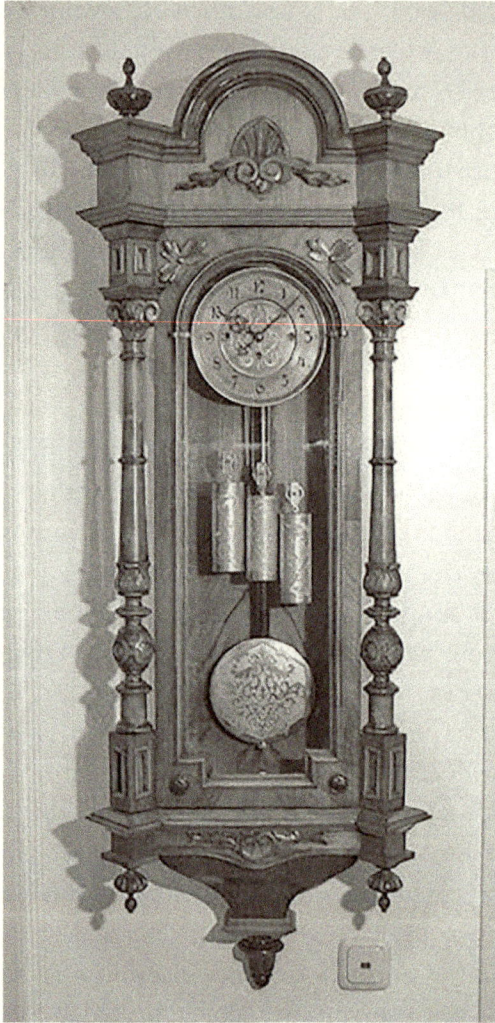

The pendulum was the key to getting accurate time from early clocks.

The first pendulum clock was produced in 1656 by the Dutch inventor Christiaan Huygens. Galileo had come up with the idea of a pendulum in 1637 as a way to keep regular time. Huygens discovered that wide pendulum swings made the pendulum inaccurate, but an anchor escapement that restricted the pendulum swing to only four to six inches resulted in much-improved accuracy. With increased accuracy, a minute hand was added to clocks beginning around 1690. The English carpenter, John Harrison, built on these principles to produce his famous chronometers in an effort to win England's "longitudinal prize" for an accurate timepiece that worked on ships. In 1761 he demonstrated his timepiece on a voyage to Jamaica in which it lost only twenty-four seconds over the nine-day sail. In the ensuing years, clocks would appear in every sphere of life. Clocks were a key to the organized workday of the Industrial Revolution, and they became part of public life—especially in train stations during the age of rail. In his diary, Samuel Pepys describes the pleasure (in 1665) of owning a novelty, a pocket watch.[186] A few years later, a novel notion came to England—the umbrella.[187]

The six more modest innovations were:

1. The safety pin
2. The tin can
3. The propeller
4. The postage stamp
5. The piano
6. Modern perforated toilet paper

A New York man invented the safety pin and received a patent in 1849. It looked exactly like the present-day safety pin. A Frenchman invented the tin can for storing food in 1810, and his idea was put to use by the British Royal Navy in 1813 to feed its sailors. The propeller has been known since ancient times. It was called Archimedes Screw when it was used to move water to a higher level, but the screw propeller was first used in the 1830s to propel boats in the water—much like present-day ocean steamers are powered by massive propellers, not to mention propeller-driven airplanes.

Prior to 1840, letters were mailed and delivered, but the receiver was responsible for paying the postage cost when the letter arrived. It was not cheap. In 1838 a letter sent from Edinburgh to London cost a shilling—almost a day's wages for a farmer or factory worker. England changed this system in 1840 when it introduced the world's first postage stamp. It cost one penny (to send a letter weighing no more than a half-ounce), and it featured an image of the twenty-one-year-old Queen Victoria. The convenience of a one-penny postage stamp spurred an explosion of correspondence in England, with the volume of letters increasing from seventy million to three hundred and fifty million in the first ten years after its introduction.[188] Soon, other European countries were issuing postage stamps and witnessing a huge increase in correspondence.

England introduced fast and inexpensive mail in 1840 featuring the young Queen Victoria on the penny stamp.

The piano, invented in about 1700 by the Italian Bartolomeo Christofori, is a relatively recent invention. He wanted a musical instrument that could play both soft and loud notes, and initially, it was called a *fortepiano* which means "loud/soft." Its predecessor was the harpsichord, but the piano was much more versatile. The new piano could sustain notes and could play with great volume. In 1800 pianos were made with cast iron frames which allowed much greater string tensions and a more powerful sound—suitable for the romantic music of the day. In the 1730s in Germany, an organ builder named Gottfried Silbermann showed his piano to Johann Sebastian Bach. Bach was not especially impressed, but he suggested that Silbermann find a way to make the high notes play with stronger volume. Silbermann incorporated Bach's ideas, and Bach became a sponsor of pianos. Mozart liked pianos and composed music for them. Soon pianos were popular in Germany.

We know that modern perforated toilet paper is a very recent invention, but once paper became cheap, it was used as toilet paper. Sources tell us that Zeth Wheeler of Albany, New York, was the first to produce inexpensive paper on rolls with perforations in 1871.

How they dressed

This period brought several key changes in clothing: underwear, big fashion changes for those who could afford new clothes, ready-made clothes began to replace homemade clothes, trousers replaced breeches, and most important, cotton became the new accessible miracle fabric.

Let's start with cotton because this new fabric revolutionized peasant clothing well before 1850.

It is worth noting the history of how cotton penetrated Europe. Cotton had been grown since ancient times in places like Egypt and India. The entry of cotton into Germany was dependent upon European trade with India, which occurred well after the medieval period. In 1599 Queen Elizabeth I chartered the British East India Company. At that time, India dominated both the growth of the cotton plant and the manufacture of cotton clothing. Cotton proved to have wonderful advantages over other fabrics. It was lightweight. It was soft (not scratchy) to the skin. It "breathed" and thus wicked away sweat and oils from one's skin. Cotton accepted dyes very well, which made it ideal for colorful clothing. Cotton was easily washable. Cotton was also versatile and could be woven into a variety of fabrics, from soft, dainty lace to tough-as-iron denim. Finally, cotton would prove to be a very inexpensive fabric. In the 1600s, it was the miracle fabric.

Germany had no direct trading access to India, so it had to depend upon the trading networks of the Dutch, the Portuguese and the English. Those countries competed for trading rights with India until England emerged as the winner. But England had a mixed reaction to cotton. England's economy was based on wool, and cotton threatened that lucrative business. Initially, the British politicians passed laws to protect wool. In fact, in 1678, the British parliament passed a law requiring that everyone must be buried in wool. They proposed other laws mandating that those living in England must wear wool six months a year, but these bills died without passing.

Calico was the cheap cotton fabric from India that was introduced to England in the 1690s.[189] It soon found a mass-market among the poor. In 1699 the Tory party in England passed a bill that forbade the importation of Indian calicoes. These were dyed cotton fabrics. This backfired. Calicoes suddenly became "forbidden fruit" and all the more desirable. For the nobility, cotton joined silk as a luxury fabric of choice. In 1721 parliament banned the importation of plain Indian cotton cloth.

Suddenly England used raw cotton as the commodity to spur its Industrial Revolution. It imported raw cotton first from India and then from the southern states of the United States. Next, England created a series of machines to spin the cotton fibers into thread and weave the cotton thread into cloth. Soon England was producing fine printed cotton fabrics (and ruining the Indian weavers).[190] By 1775 cotton garments had become extremely popular, and they migrated from England east toward Russia. Soon Europe was flooded with cotton sheets, cotton tablecloths, cotton underwear, cotton sacks, cotton trousers for peasants, and cotton sailcloth for sailing ships. By 1805 cotton fabrics accounted for 42 percent of all British exports, and inexpensive cotton clothing was being sold in Germany and all over Europe.[191]

Cotton singlehandedly changed dress habits. Beginning in 1750, men began to wear cotton underdrawers, which they changed and washed daily.[192] Women resisted this trend toward underpants. Instead, they stayed with the ankle or knee-length chemise or shift (the modern-day "slip"). The chemise previously had been made of linen, but with the arrival of cotton, a cotton chemise was preferred because it was soft and "wicked away" body moisture. It was not until the 1820s that women began to wear cotton underpants. The bra was a much later invention. Some historians claim that bras were worn in the Middle Ages, but most agree that the bra was not invented until 1913, when Mary Phelps Jacobs asked her maid to attach two handkerchiefs with ribbon and a strap to create a bra for a fancy dance. Ms. Jacobs went on to patent her invention. Until that time, women wore either a tight corset (covering them from breasts to hips) in order to reduce their waistline to twenty-one inches or, like most poor women, they simply wore a loose-fitting chemise.

Prior to 1800, virtually all peasant clothing was "homespun." Each garment was either sewn by the mother of the household or else it was sewn by a relative, friend or neighbor and acquired through barter. This was the established practice ever since the Iron Age. Cotton began to change this practice because cotton made it possible to manufacture inexpensive ready-made clothes. Various simple garments were mass-produced in factories—underwear, shirts, blouses, socks. These items were so inexpensive that peasants could afford to buy them. This meant that after 1800 German peasants began to wear store-bought clothes for the first time. This was a worldwide phenomenon. The first ready-made clothing factory opened in New York in 1831.[193]

An even more significant change in how peasants dressed was the appearance of trousers. Until well into the 1700s, peasant men continued to wear long hose up to the knee and then breeches from the knee to the waist. (Think of tight-fitting knickers.) They wore a simple shirt or jacket above the waist. But during the French Revolution of 1789, French men began to adopt trousers, which were radically new in three ways.

1. They were loose as opposed to the skin-tight hose or breeches.
2. They were ankle-length where breeches had generally been knee-length for the previous two hundred years.
3. They were open at the bottom; breeches were fastened at the knee.[194]

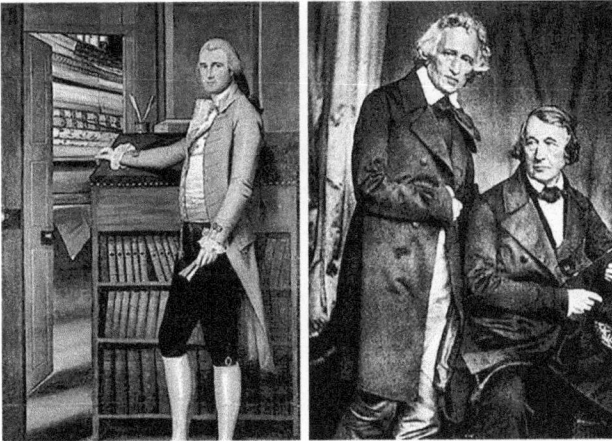

Left: This painting shows a gentleman wearing breeches in 1789—the last period before trousers came into vogue. Right: This image of the Grimm brothers from 1854 shows them wearing the newly fashionable trousers.

Protection against the rain came much later. Although the umbrella had been in use around the world since ancient times, its introduction to northern Europe was surprisingly late. In the 1730s, an English gentleman named John Hanway created a scandal and was mocked when he began carrying an umbrella on the streets of London, and very slowly, other men began to imitate him, carrying their own "Hanway"—later called an "umbrella." The true raincoat came even later. In 1823 Charles Macintosh used his chemical skills to treat fabrics to make them waterproof. His rainproof coat was quickly described as a "Macintosh." It's unlikely that either of these inventions, umbrellas or Macintoshes, were used by our German peasant ancestors before 1850.

Bathing and grooming

It is clear that during this time, the German peasants took more care of their grooming and appearance. One aspect of this grooming was the increased importance of mirrors. We have seen that glass technology—especially sheet glass—improved significantly in 1650 with the technology to cast large sheets of flat glass.[195] This made it possible to manufacture mirrors. By 1650 mirrors were important not only for grooming but also for surveying and navigational instruments. The necessary reflecting surface was made of thin sheets of tin in 1650. It was not until after 1850 that true silvering was invented—that is, depositing a bright film of metallic silver on glass by chemical methods.

Another change affected hairstyles. There are reports that beards had been common for men until about 1700. During his long reign from 1643 to 1715, Louis XIV set the tone for style in France and throughout Europe. He was clean-shaven, and the nobility imitated this all over Europe. It seems probable that much of the peasantry eventually followed the model of the local nobleman. This meant that most peasant men were clean-shaven until about 1800, when Romanticism first blossomed, especially in Germany, and Romanticism brought back beards.[196] Beards were firmly in style from 1800 to 1920 and the end of World War I. However, we must be cautious about suggesting that all German peasant men adopted the fashions of the day. It seems quite likely that many peasants followed the habits of hundreds of years: they occasionally shaved, perhaps weekly, so that their face was usually covered with a thick five o'clock shadow.

We have hints of what might have been the most significant change in bathing and grooming—the beginnings of a "bathroom." Until about 1800, peasants relieved themselves using a chamber pot indoors and using a version of an "outhouse" out of doors. These chamber pots were stored and used in the common room of the house both day and night. With prosperity, some peasants were able to afford larger houses. In some homes, there were multiple bedchambers, in which case each bedchamber had its own chamber pot.[197] In contrast, the expression "without a pot to piss in" was a vulgar term used to describe the poorest families who did not own a chamber pot but simply used the outdoors at all times and seasons. By 1820 chamber pots were cheap enough that virtually all families could afford one. The task of gathering, emptying and cleaning the chamber pots was a daily task in each family.

By 1850 the flushing toilet was just over the horizon. In fact, in 1851, London hosted "The Great Exhibition of the Works of Industry of all Nations," where twenty-five countries contributed exhibits of their state-of-the-art technology. The Crystal Palace in Hyde Park was the main exhibition hall and was equipped with flushing toilets that the public could use for the price of one penny. These toilets were a novelty and a huge success. Of the six million people who attended the exhibit, over six hundred thousand paid one penny to use a flushing toilet. At the end of the summer, the Crystal Palace was removed, but the plumber who installed the toilets convinced the organizers to keep them open. They agreed, and these public flushing toilets generated over one thousand pounds sterling each year and spurred London to establish more public toilets across the city.[198]

Washing oneself was done without any privacy. Many washed outside at their doors or at the public wells closest to their houses. Because they were washing outdoors in full view of others, they usually washed only their hands and face each day.[199] A full-body sponge bath traditionally took place near the fire in the family's main room. Many peasant men and women washed without soap which was reserved for laundering clothes. Instead, they used a brisk rubbing with a coarse towel to scrub off the dirt. Gradually the practice of complete bathing was spreading. The person would undress completely and sponge bath their entire body, including their private parts.

The full-body bathing triggered the beginnings of a "bathroom" as we know it. As historian Jack Larkin explains, "Families began to move washing equipment out of kitchens and into bedchambers, thus moving from shared space to a space that could be made private. As more prosperous households furnished one or two of their bed chambers with washing equipment—a washstand, a basin and a large-mouth pitcher—family members could shut the chamber door, undress and wash themselves completely."[200] From this arrangement, it would be a small step to dedicate one room in the house as a combination bathing room and the chamber pot room. There was no running water, of course, but at least the individual enjoyed a few moments of privacy for their most personal activities.

Travel and transportation

There was inertia in many aspects of life, including travel and transportation, between 1400 and 1800. "Overland transport, very early possessed the elements which could have led to its being perfected. And slowly, we see faster speeds being reached because modern roads were built or because vehicles carrying goods and passengers were improved or new staging posts were established. But progress of this kind only became widespread by about 1830, which was just before the railway revolution."[201] It has been famously observed by the twentieth-century French philosopher Paul Valery when he said, "Napoleon moved no faster than Julius Caesar."[202] In fact, Julius Caesar often led his army along excellent Roman roads—far superior to the roads of Europe between 1650 and 1850. However, some historians believe that in the late 1700s, there were German officials who remained ambivalent about improving roads and bridges, fearing that good roads could serve as an open invitation to invading armies.

There are vivid eyewitness accounts of the problems of travel between 1800 and 1830.[203] The journey of 138 miles from Frankfurt to Stuttgart took forty-six hours riding a post wagon—exactly three miles an hour. Another traveler wrote, "We were scarcely out of Hanover (in 1828) and the wheels already drowned in sand up to the axletree; tedium to the eye and death to the patience of the traveler with the added vexation of paying tolls for permission to follow the most convenient track."[204] As late as 1850, the roads in Bavaria were described as "very bad" and "the usual speed of a journey could be no more than one German mile an hour." In contrast to Bavaria, Prussia was the example of a progressive and modern state. They began a serious program of building hard surface roads in 1816 when they had only four thousand miles of such improved roads, but by 1852 they had almost ten thousand miles of hard surface roads.[205]

In 1690 when something was not especially heavy (in other words, a letter or small package), and it was urgent to get it delivered quickly, the Germans developed and used a novel transport system—human runners. These were men who carried a satchel and their trademark water bottle. It is said that they left the main roads and took shortcuts. They wore distinctive running shoes and attached bells to their belts—ostensibly to keep them awake. For a time, this was a family occupation. Fathers taught their sons how to run long distances beginning at the age of seven. At times they ran in a network of relays, with each runner covering about two leagues (six miles) before handing off the package to the next runner. The package could be transported thirty to sixty miles in a day.[206]

We saw that the four-wheel cart with a pivoting front axle was the major invention of 1450 to 1650. The pivoting front axle also facilitated the introduction of the stagecoach in the period from 1650 to 1850. Stagecoaches for travelers only appeared in the Romantic period beginning about 1800.[207] Stagecoaches were famous for being fast as well as dangerous. They were tippy, accidents were common and no one compensated the victims. The worst problem was that the roads were not built for them. If two stagecoaches met going in opposite directions, they could not pass without a wheel plunging into the mud at the side of the road.

The first known European stagecoach route was started in 1610—a twelve-mile route to connect Edinburgh with Leith in Scotland. By 1650 stagecoaches were beginning to appear throughout Europe as well as at the coaching inns along the routes. Stagecoaches carried six passengers plus two drivers and were pulled by a team of four to six horses. They averaged about five miles an hour and covered sixty to seventy miles in a day.

Key improvements in the design of stagecoaches began immediately. The first spring-suspended coaches appeared in the 1660s.[208] These were C-shaped strips of tempered steel.[209] Spoked wheels with iron rim brakes were introduced soon thereafter. The key benefit was that the stagecoach traveled on a set schedule. These stagecoaches were quickly adopted by the postal service to carry letters. Stagecoaches spurred the building of coaching inns and the improvement of roads. But hills were a chronic challenge. Men would get out and push the coach going up steep hills, and when racing down a steep hill, everyone held on for dear life.

Travel was slow and sleeping accommodations on the road were quite crude. It seems the facilities were mostly devoted to the horses. One source explains, "Inns in 1693 were described as nothing but long stables where the horses occupy the central part, the sides are left for the Masters." As if to contrast the poor facilities with superior travel accommodations in foreign countries, the historian Fernand Braudel goes on to say, "In Persia, a good caravanserai was found every four leagues (a league equals three miles).[210]

An illustration of a stagecoach adapted as a Post Coach in Switzerland.

The new stagecoach created a need for improved roads using the newly invented macadam.

A further burden for the traveler was the profusion of toll gates at kingdom borders. The toll keeper and his family lived in a small house connected to the gate itself. Someone appeared twenty-four hours a day to collect the toll before lifting the gate. Tolls were charged for both passengers and for goods.

The revolution in transportation rested on coal. Great quantities of coal were required to fuel the steam-powered engines for trains and ships. But this presented a sort of "chicken and egg" quandary. Before the availability of steam engines, it was very difficult to transport coal. In fact, until the appearance of coal-fired railways trains in the mid-1800s, "the major obstacle to the spread of coal was indeed transport over land, usually effected by carts or pack animals."[211]

"Around 1840, when sailing ships and steamships existed side by side, it was estimated that steam did the work of about five sailing ships of equal tonnage."[212] Coal was the key to the transportation revolution of the 1840s for both steamships and steam-powered locomotives.

Canals were another important breakthrough in this period. We previously mentioned the chronic problems of land transport ("mud and bandits"), but we should add a third—cost. Shipping something overland was not only time-consuming it was also very expensive. For example, in the 1600s, a cask of wine cost forty Francs at the vineyard in Beaune. But the cost of shipping the cask to Paris overland, a distance of 180 miles, added an additional one hundred Francs to the cost in Paris. In the early 1700s, the packhorse was still the prime goods carrier, but the cost of using packhorses to ship freight overland was extremely expensive. Coal carried from Newcastle to London by packhorse cost six times its pithead price when delivered in London. As late as 1828, Americans living along the Atlantic coast would warm themselves with coal from England, three thousand miles across the ocean, rather than seek firewood from the inland forests just thirty miles away.[213]

The speed and relative safety of water travel inspired innovators to introduce water travel across land. They did this by digging canals. We know that in America, the Erie Canal was an instant success when it was finished in 1825. In Europe, the 1830s was the golden age of canal building. Of course, the first obstacle to linking two cities with a canal is the technology to build locks to allow ships to navigate changes in elevation. The first German canal with locks was the Stecknitz Canal, which allowed commerce to cross from the North Sea to the Baltic without the long and dangerous strait between Copenhagen, Denmark and Malmo, Sweden. The canal was only seven miles long, but it provided a link to connect Lauenburg and Lubeck for transporting salt. It was completed in 1398. By the 1830s, Germany was honeycombed with canals linking some of its main rivers—the Elbe, Oder and Weser.

Water travel on rivers also improved greatly with the introduction of the steamer. By 1846 there were 180 steamers working the German rivers. Prior to the steamer, it was often necessary to tow a boat upstream using both men and animals at a rate of about two miles per hour.

We have seen the interesting improvements in overland transportation with the development of stagecoach routes and the growing network of canals, but both of these innovations were suddenly made obsolete by the first truly revolutionary change in transportation in two thousand years—the coal-fired steam engine.

The beginnings of the German railway system date back to the late 1700s, when mines began to use wagonways to pull coal out of the mines. These mines were located in the industrial Ruhr valley. A pair of iron rails were laid on the ground, and a team of horses would pull a wagon along the rails. This "iron way" created the German name *Eisenbahn*, which is used today to describe modern German railroads. These wagonways expanded, but they were solely used for freight, never for passengers.[214]

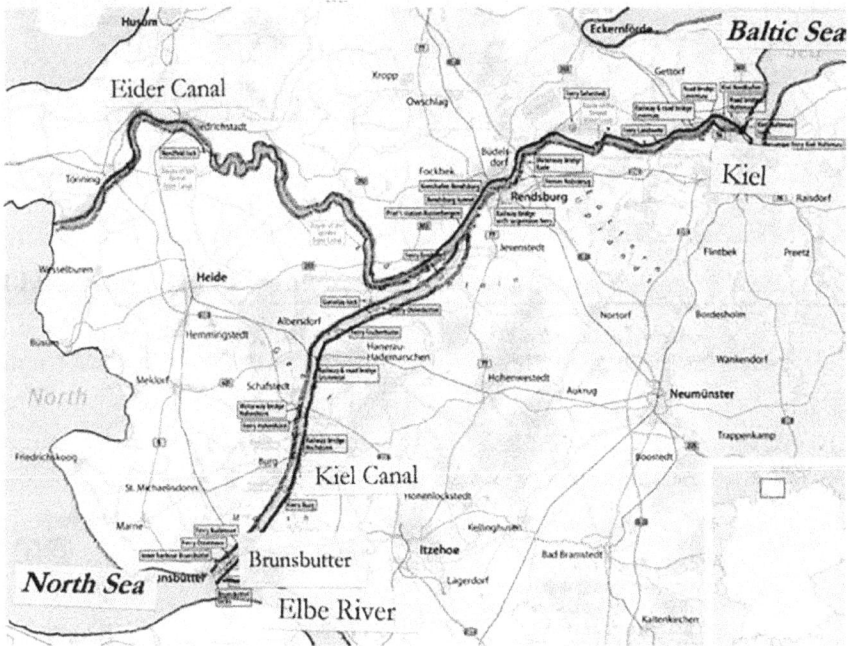

Other canals were designed to carve a short cut for ships to move between the North Sea and the Baltic Sea. The Eider Canal took a northern route and was completed in 1784 followed by the Kiel Canal completed in 1895.

**The first railway in the German lands opened in 1835
to connect Nuremberg with Furth.**

Steam-powered locomotives debuted in England in the early 1800s, but there were two obstacles to their adoption in Germany. First, the German lands were so divided in the 1820s that it was difficult to lay down a railway without infringing on a "foreign land." Second, the nobility favored canal projects over railways because they were viewed as more prestigious. It was the liberal middle class (the same people who gathered to plan a new government in Frankfurt in 1848) who supported railways as a progressive innovation that would benefit all the German people.

Most historians consider the first railway in Germany to be the twenty-three-mile line connecting Furth and Nuremberg, which opened in 1835. The great event was celebrated with ceremonial canons and the music of a brass band.[215] It was powered by a coal-fired steam locomotive built in Newcastle, England. It could reach a top speed of twenty to thirty miles per hour. This speed was frightening to many, but the railroad proved its utility. Soon longer rail lines were being built all over Germany. In 1846 the last section was completed in the 178-mile line linking Berlin and Hamburg.

We can see the remarkable growth of railroad traffic after 1850 by comparing it to other methods of carrying freight. The historian James J. Sheehan reports, "In 1850 shipping on rivers, canals, and overland carried three times the freight as carried by railroads. By 1870 railroads had a lead of almost four to one."[216]

Table talk: The stagecoach trip

Carl and Charlotte are a young married couple living in the 1820s in a small town near the city of Freiburg in the Black Forest. Charlotte's uncle, Walter, has written them to report that he is coming to visit them from his home one hundred miles to the north. He is interested in shopping for a supplier of Black Forest cuckoo clocks for his store. He says he would like to visit them when he arrives. Carl has never met him, and Charlotte has not seen him since she was a little girl. Her father told her he owns a successful store. They greet him at the front door and welcome him in. He is a large, heavy-set man with a beard, and a big smile. Charlotte offers him a glass of beer which he enthusiastically accepts. Carl joins him at the table with his beer while Charlotte begins preparing a snack of bread, cheese and sausage. They want to be good hosts.

Carl: "How was your trip?"

Walter: "Exhausting. I thought it would never end."

Carl: "How long did it take?"

Walter: "Let's see. I am told the total distance was about 150 kilometers, and it took us three days."

Carl: "You can't walk 150 kilometers in three days."

Walter: "Oh, no. I took the coach."

Carl: "Oh, you traveled in the new stagecoach. I have seen it in town delivering passengers at the Boar's Head Inn, but I don't think I know anyone who has ridden in it. What was it like?"

Walter: "Well, where do I begin? I met the coach in my hometown in the market square. I waited about an hour. It was running late. I got a seat in the middle facing backward, so that became my seat for the journey. The coach seats six people inside. Three face forward and three face backward. The only seat left was in the middle facing backward.

There were two married couples and one other man already seated. I am not a small man, and I was squeezed . . . well, we were all squeezed in together. My traveling bag was put up on top of the coach. There we sat, crammed together like a school of herring."

Carl: "How was the ride?"

Walter: "Bumpy, very bumpy. I understand these new coaches have springs, but it was still very bumpy going over that terrible road. We were pulled by two horses. The men were asked to get out and walk alongside when we went up an especially steep hill. But the worst part was going downhill. I thought we might run out of control."

Carl: "Where did you get food?"

Walter: "We stopped at lunchtime at an inn and had some soup. Well, we actually stopped a lot. We must have gone through a dozen toll gates—stopping to pay the toll each time."

Charlotte: "You said it took three days, Uncle Walter. Did you travel all night?"

Walter: "No. No. We stopped at an inn each night, had a big supper of bratwurst each evening, and I shared a bed with the other fellow who was traveling in the coach. That wasn't too bad."

Carl: "How far did you travel each day?"

Walter: "Well, we were on the road for about ten hours each day, and I think we covered about 50 kilometers on average. Occasionally the horses trotted, but other times they slowed to a crawl to go over the worst potholes. So, I suppose we averaged about five kilometers per hour. About as fast as you might walk. There were openings for windows but no glass. We all appreciated the fresh air coming in through those windows, but when it rained this afternoon, we pulled the curtains tight to keep out the rain. We managed."

Charlotte: "Uncle, are you returning the same way?"

Walter: "Yes, but I learned a few things from my first trip. First, I will tip the coach driver and make sure I get a seat by the window and facing forward. Second, I will bring along some food and something to drink in the coach. Third, I will pay a little extra to get a room and a bed to myself. Well, enough about me. Tell me how you two have been. And how is my brother doing?"

Family

As in every previous period, the family was the most supportive institution in one's everyday life after 1650. "The family was supposed to provide the first and most reliable line of defense against the world outside. But the family was anything but stable. Families were continually disrupted by death, usually of children, but also of one or both parents. Moreover, in most families, childhood was brief. Boys and girls of twelve or thirteen often had to leave home to work."[217]

"In contrast to its modern counterpart, therefore, the traditional family was more apt to be shaped by trade regulations, land tenure patterns and inheritance laws than by sexual attraction and personal satisfaction. It was an economic rather than an emotional unit."[218]

Because marriage was an economic unit, as late as the 1800s, one required some means of production, usually land or the right to practice a trade, in order to start a household.[219] As the population increased and land became more scarce, this hard fact produced the "European marriage pattern" in which most people married fairly late in life. For example, in one typical German village, first marriages occurred at twenty-nine or thirty years of age in the early 1800s. Almost half of the women and more than half of the men would still be unmarried at age thirty-five, and of these, a significant number would remain single for life. They were "forced to live their entire lives tending other people's fields, cleaning other people's houses and nurturing other people's children."[220]

In fact, most households needed two active adults to function properly. This meant that second and sometimes third marriages were required so that the surviving partner might keep the household intact. Consequently, the stepmother was a familiar figure in traditional folk literature.

The high incidence of mortality for mothers during childbirth created a pattern of widowers as old as forty looking for younger stepmothers. It was an arrangement that benefited both parties. The widower desperately needed a partner to take care of his house and his children, as well as tend the kitchen garden and help in the fields at harvest time. The young woman might have no dowry and few other prospects.

It was common for an older man to marry a younger woman, especially after the untimely death of the first or second wife.

It is striking to note that the weakening of social controls in German communities had the side effect of a dramatic increase in illegitimacy, which was an unusual demographic phenomenon that occurred throughout Europe. It had been rare, but illegitimacy in some areas became more and more common after 1750. The number of illegitimate births per 100 live births grew from less than three before 1750 to 12 between 1780 and 1820. In the same periods, pre-marital conceptions went from 13.4 per 1,000 to 23.8.[221] The prospects for an illegitimate child were dim. Destitute pregnant women gravitated to cities to have their babies. The death rate was shocking. Almost half of those born illegitimately in Berlin did not reach their first birthday.[222]

Although the factory system appeared in Europe in the 1800s, child labor was an essential part of traditional economic life—not an invention of the factory system.[223]

Arthur E. Imhof, a professor of social history at the Free University of Berlin, gives us a very interesting perspective of the German family from 1650 to the present. In his book, *Lost Worlds,* he argues that the world view of a number of German families was quite different from the contemporary world view (German or American). He points out that the classic German prayer—one that was prayed countless times during this time period was, "Protect us, oh Lord, from plague, famine and war."

Imhof explains that life was uncertain and filled with sudden dangers. As a coping mechanism, several German people focused on what they could control. They had little control over their own individual life, so they poured their energies into preserving something they could control—the family name and family farm. This was especially true in those parts of the German lands which practiced impartible inheritance and thus had larger farms.

He meticulously researched the story of the family of Johannes Hooss and the 106-acre "Valtes Farm" in northern Hesse. First, we learn that this farm has been passed on through the generations intact to this present day. It has never been divided, and not a single acre has ever been sold. Second, through multiple generations, from 1584 to 1945, the farm was passed down to someone named Hooss, and in ten of the eleven cases, his name was Johannes Hooss. To ensure that Johannes Hooss will run the farm in perpetuity, the family often named multiple sons Johannes—as many as five sons in one generation—all to ensure that there would be a survivor named Johannes Hooss who could take over the farm. Third, the family's focus was always to be good stewards of this farm. It was maintained and improved through the years, a source of great family pride. This prosperous farm became a family heirloom—highly prized by everyone in the family—including those who would never inherit it. The farm was prestigious, and it always served to attract excellent marriage candidates from other villages for the eventual young man who would take over the farm. But it also helped the daughters in the family to marry into similarly prestigious farm families.[224]

In summary, instead of the typical American world view of individualism, many German families in this period focused on investing and preserving the family farm. All family members saw themselves as temporarily filling a role in preserving the precious Valtes Farm.

Health and medical care

By 1650 the most feared diseases had evolved. Tuberculosis is an ancient disease, but it flourished beginning around 1800 when people became crowded into filthy cities. Soon five hundred people out of every one hundred thousand were dying of tuberculosis each year in European cities.[225] Tuberculosis was often called "consumption." In the popular imagination, it was especially tragic because it appeared to single out attractive young women—think of the tragic Mimi in Puccini's 1896 opera *La Boheme*.[226]

People who lacked sufficient protein in their diets and lived in unsanitary and crowded conditions were the most vulnerable. The correct diagnosis and cure would have to wait until 1882, when Dr. Robert Koch in Germany discovered the bacillus that caused tuberculosis. Koch and Louis Pasteur would change the world of medicine through their discoveries in bacteriology.

Smallpox was a terrible disease that scarred and killed its victims. In the 1760s, safer methods of inoculation were being developed, and in 1796 Edward Jenner introduced a safe cowpox vaccination in England.[227] It spread across Europe very quickly. Soon doctors took to the road to offer a traveling clinic from town to town, offering smallpox vaccinations to all who came to the clinic. The smallpox vaccination was an early and rare treatment breakthrough.

A doctor surrounded by mothers with children waiting to be vaccinated.

Typhus played a substantial role in turning Napoleon's 1812 expedition to Russia into a catastrophe.[228] Cholera, however, was easily the biggest epidemic news of the nineteenth century. In 1831 there was a pandemic of cholera that started in Asia, spread to Russia and then to Europe. These cholera pandemics persisted. They returned in 1854 and again in 1863.[229] Cholera was extremely infectious, and the root cause, a bacterium called Vibrio cholera, was first isolated in 1883 by the German physician Robert Koch.

Gout was another disease of this period. Its typical symptom was a painful big toe. During this time, it was believed that diseases were territorial. If you had one disease, it would ward off other diseases. Gout was seen as a rich man's disease caused by excessive drinking and eating rich food. Some wealthy men seemed happy to have the disease because it was not fatal, and it might make them immune to diseases that were fatal.[230] Cancer, heart-related ailments and probably Alzheimer's disease are ancient diseases of humankind, but prior to 1850 people seldom lived long enough to acquire them.[231]

Genuine breakthroughs were rare before 1850, but let's look at some examples. In 1785, an English doctor, William Withering, promoted the benefits of digitalis (found in the foxglove plant) for heart problems. He credited a folk healer who "first fixed my attention on the foxglove."[232]

A second breakthrough was the microscope invented in 1673 by the Dutchman Antony van Leeuwenhoek.[233] He taught himself how to grind, polish and mount lenses of considerable magnifying power. He was the first person to see living protozoa and bacteria under a lens. He wrote reports for the Royal Society of his findings, and for fifty years, people traveled to his home in Delft to look through his lenses. The scientific elite made a series of breakthroughs between 1680 and 1720, and these scientific discoveries were slowly put into practical application in the years to follow.

In the early 1600s, an English doctor, William Harvey, traveled to Italy to study at Padua. He was the first to conclude that blood circulated around the body using a system of valves. This was one of those scientific discoveries that paved the way for later applications.[234] Indeed, it was after his lifetime that others learned how the blood got from the arteries to the veins. This was discovered in 1661 using microscopes to discover capillaries.

Although there were scientific advances, the actual practice of medicine had changed very little in the thousand years leading up to 1800. However, this is when science began to make inroads into medicine. Prior to 1800, almost all theorizing about the mechanisms of disease was like a castle built in the air. The theories had little empirical foundation.[235] Beginning around 1780, a series of medical breakthroughs appeared that finally produced accurate diagnoses and then wondrous cures. But the progress was slow and difficult. It was difficult because the experts had to "unlearn" the traditional ideas. Until about 1870, to be a surgeon or a "medical man" meant bloodletting.[236] Traditional treatments were dying out grudgingly. Therefore, throughout much of the world, traditional medical therapeutics amounted to making patients anemic through bloodletting, depleting them of fluids and valuable electrolytes via laxatives and poisoning them with compounds of such heavy metals like mercury and lead. In fact, in 1755, one physician in the United States warned that "there is more danger from the physician than from the distemper."[237]

Poor nutrition made people vulnerable to many diseases, so the introduction of the potato contributed to protecting people because the potato was easy to grow even in colder climates, and it provided abundant calories along with nutrients in the form of vitamins and minerals.[238]

In about 1750, it was discovered that citrus juice would prevent scurvy. British sailors were regularly issued lime juice—hence acquiring the nickname "Limey."[239] The German physician F. Anton Mesmer (1734–1815) introduced hypnotism, and he used it effectively in his medical practice.[240]

A huge breakthrough was introduced in Vienna in 1847 when Dr. Ignaz Semmelweis noticed that doctors were coming directly from the morgue to the maternity ward to deliver babies. The rate of deaths from puerperal fever was as high as 30 percent. In some cases, the mothers also died agonizing deaths. Dr. Semmelweis ran the maternity ward, and in 1847 he insisted that each doctor wash his hands in a chlorine solution before entering the ward. The deaths from puerperal fever immediately dropped by 90 percent. The protocol of hand washing spread quickly in the medical community, and this contributed to the "medical revolution" of the 1860s.[241]

The tide of public opinion turned against the ancient practice of examining and tasting a patient's urine. Although this was still a trademark of a physician, the image of a doctor holding up a flask of urine had become an object of ridicule after 1650.[242] Soon, urine-gazing became the mark of a quack.

During the 1600s, scorn was poured on the "humor" theories which were finally dismissed as empty verbiage.[243] This represented progress, of course, but this theory was replaced in the 1700s with the popular "miasma theory." The miasma was identified as the "exhalations" given off by stagnant ponds, rotting vegetables, animal waste, human waste and anything that was filthy and putrescent. The theory was one way to explain why the slums of cities were often most severely stricken during an epidemic. This theory seemed to have a link to soil and the environment, and thus it had the appearance of being more scientific than the humor theory. Although this miasma theory was wrong, it served a positive purpose because its antidote was sanitation.[244]

In the years before 1850, doctors were surprisingly ineffective in healing people. But even if modern doctors could not cure their patients, at least an understanding of disease mechanisms and drug action kept them from doing harm. So doctors in the 1800s began to interview the patient to get a full history, then they conducted a physical examination, seeking to pin down the nature of the problem. Doctors also palpated the patient's abdomen and percussed the chest, with their ear pressed to the body before the appearance of the stethoscope. The stethoscope was invented in 1816 in France by Dr. Rene Laennec, who was uncomfortable placing his ear on a woman's chest to hear her heartbeat.[245] It soon became the new "trademark" of a doctor—a man in a clean white coat with a stethoscope hanging from his neck.[246] The stethoscope became the most important medical instrument of the period until the introduction of x-rays in the 1890s.

Homeopathic medicine was born in Germany in about 1800 when Dr. Christian Hahnemann concluded that if the cinchona bark with its ingredient of quinine can cure those who have malaria, it will be beneficial to healthy people in small doses. He researched and built a collection of herbal remedies for various ailments, which he sold through apothecaries.[247]

We have pointed out that although a doctor's bag held a number of medicines, very few did any good. In fact, when *Pharmacopoeia* was published in London, listing hundreds of medicines, only two offered relief. One was a deep brownish ingredient mixed with alcohol and called "opium." It was swallowed for pain relief. The second was foxglove, which contains digitalis that, in turn, stimulates the kidneys to make urine. As late as 1850, there was nothing to prevent infectious diseasest, cancer, arthritis, diabetes, asthma or heart attacks.[248] To be fair, there were some things that doctors could do: relieve suffering, set bones, sew up cuts and open boils.[249]

What about tooth care? Tooth care was still extremely primitive at the end of this period. A toothbrush with bristles was invented in England in the 1770s and was mass-produced as early as 1780. A German dentist introduced novocaine in 1905. Porcelain crowns appeared in 1903, and the number of people who brushed their teeth each day slowly increased. The almanacs of the period gave detailed instructions on how to brush your teeth. Extraction of a diseased tooth was a well-established practice, and it was a decisive and a relatively safe procedure.

Birth control was practiced in many parts of Germany in a fashion that skirted around the Catholic prohibitions. A 1761 report from Berlin told of women nursing their children to age two or even three. Women had become aware that they rarely became pregnant while nursing.[250]

In terms of health outcomes, we see reports that between 1770 and 1820, European adults were, on average, noticeably shorter than previous generations. The problem was insufficient food.[251] The single best indicator of the quality of medicine and health care in any age is the life expectancy at birth. There are indications that during the Iron Age in Germany, the life expectancy at birth was about twenty-six years. We find that from 1770 to 1875, the life expectancy at birth remained steady at thirty-five years.[252] Only after 1875 was there an increase.

People who did reach their forties or fifties looked old. A forty-five-year-old might have white hair, a bent back and a face as wrinkled as an eighty-year-old today. A thirty-year-old woman might be called "Old Gretel."[253] By 1900, life expectancy at birth rose to forty-two, and in 1950 it had jumped to sixty-five. As of 2015, the life expectancy at birth in Germany was eighty-one years. Human life expectancy has increased far more in the last one hundred years than it did in the previous two thousand years.

Hardly any eighteenth-century scientific advance helped heal the sick directly, so the net contribution of physicians to the relief and cure of the sick remained marginal. In about 1875, doctors were able to diagnose disease scientifically while they remained powerless therapeutically.[254]

A review of some important medical breakthroughs that took place after 1850

Before 1850 doctors worked alone or with the help of a haphazardly trained assistant. But the Crimean War of 1854 brought to the world Florence Nightingale, and she almost singlehandedly created the nursing profession.

Perhaps the most important discovery in diagnosis was Koch's discovery of the bacillus that caused tuberculosis. His scientific methods practiced by his followers led to the identification of the bacteria for many diseases. Koch in Germany was a rival to Louis Pasteur in France. They did not cooperate with each other, but cumulatively they made the first discoveries in medical bacteriology. The first successful demonstration of using anesthesia did not occur until 1846 in Boston. Until then, surgery was very rare. The surgeon had to be quick—completing the surgery in two minutes maximum. The surgeon also needed a very thick skin to proceed amid the screams of the patient.

The microscope reached university medicine in the 1840s, and the thermometer was put into use to measure one's fever in the 1850s.[255] By 1880, the thermometer was a standard part of the doctor's bag. The X-ray was first used by a physician in Wurzburg in 1895. The blood pressure cuff was invented in Italy in 1896. It took a little longer for medical science to recognize the importance of the comfort and confidence of the patient, but a 1924 doctor's guide admonished, "It is often very satisfying to the sick to be allowed to tell, in their own way, whatever they deem important for you to know."[256] Doctors began to listen to their patients.

Aspirin was introduced in 1899 in Germany by Bayer as a pain reliever, and it quickly became a very popular prescription in Europe and the United States. It not only brought pain relief, but it reduced fever and inflammation.[257] At the time, doctors were mystified by fever, so they focused on bringing down the fever rather than curing the infection. Bayer created barbital and began marketing it in 1903 as a sedative to induce sleep and relieve anxiety. Nitroglycerine was discovered in 1879 and found to be useful in dilating the arteries of the heart for patients experiencing angina pain.[258]

Then in 1891, an antitoxin was developed against diphtheria in the German laboratory of Robert Koch. The next year a vaccine was introduced to guard against diphtheria. This was a huge breakthrough, and it sharply upgraded the doctor's image in the eyes of the public.[259]

The delivery of medical care was made much more efficient when the first telephone exchange was connected in Hartford, Connecticut. The physician was able to speak directly to the family of the patient to assess the symptoms and determine the seriousness of the situation.

The challenge of infectious diseases was helped enormously with the 1935 appearance of sulfa drugs to be followed within ten years by the miracle drug of penicillin.[260]

Warfare and weaponry

"After 1648, there were wars of succession that embroiled many German aristocratic families. Some rulers made use of the argument that a more or less permanent state of warfare required a standing army. To support a standing army, a ruler needed money which, in turn, required an efficient means of raising taxes."[261] Therefore, increasing militarization brought increased government bureaucracy and control. Sources disagree on the exact date, but all agree that Prussia was the first German state to institute conscription. The country was divided into districts, and each district had to meet its quota. Villagers were liable for conscription up to the age of thirty-six, and they served for ten years, although most conscripts were on active duty only for a few months each summer. Those between twenty and thirty-five were eligible to be called. One could avoid service by hiring a substitute. It was common for single men to be drafted first, and to avoid the draft, some youths married at an early age—sometimes fourteen or fifteen, and their parents provided them with small plots of land.[262]

The province of Hesse-Kassel carried this conscription idea event further. Beginning in 1677, treaties were made in which Hesse-Kassel "leased out" troops to other foreign powers, first to Denmark, then to Venice, and finally to England and Holland.[263] Other provincial rulers in the German lands had tried to improve their inadequate finances in this manner, but Hesse did this on a grand scale. In 1775 the landgrave of Hesse-Kassel, Prince Friedrich II, made an agreement with King George III to provide thirty thousand Hessian soldiers to fight against the Americans as "Hessians" in the Revolutionary War. Prince Friedrich II received payment of the equivalent of three hundred million dollars today and used some of the money to build himself a castle.

Another key change was the introduction of the ring bayonet. It seems like an obvious solution, but it was slow in coming. The first use of bayonets with rifles was with "plug bayonets," which fitted snugly into the muzzle of the rifle. These appeared in the 1670s, but their big disadvantage was that with the bayonet stuck down the barrel of the rifle, there was no way to continue shooting. Therefore in 1700, the ring bayonet was invented.[264] The ring bayonet was attached firmly to the barrel (usually under the barrel) with the point extending out beyond the muzzle of the gun. It allowed an infantryman to defend himself immediately after firing. In Germany, the Great Elector introduced the paper cartridge (containing powder and shot) to his army in 1670, and this served to speed up the firing rate.[265]

The ring bayonet made the early musket much more versatile.

"Frederick the Great showed his brilliance in the Seven Years' War (1756–1763) when he employed an offensive strategy (in an era in which defense was usually emphasized). He introduced light, horse-drawn guns, which could be moved from place to place during the course of battle. In a series of battles, he defeated the Swedish, then the French, next the Russians and finally the Austrians."[266] The stunning military victories of

Napoleon in the early 1800s were not the result of technological advances. His armies fought with smooth bore muskets, swords and lances. His victories were credited to: 1. Superior numbers. He led 180,000 troops into an early battle. 2. The spirit and organization of the men who did the fighting. Napoleon was able to raise mass armies through conscription according to the famous law of August 23, 1793, which decreed that all Frenchmen are on permanent requisition for military service.[267]

The attitude of the German rulers of the day is telling. They thought it was politically dangerous to hand out muskets to their peasants. One ruler was quoted as saying, "I would rather pay my last ecu to the Elector of Saxony to have a couple of his good regiments march . . . than to arm five hundred of my peasants."[268]

In 1800 the smaller German states remained defenseless because they were small and fragmented and reluctant to forge an alliance with either Prussia or Vienna. They feared that these two larger German states would swallow them up. One German prince remarked, "One fears the French less than these two powers, and one generally finds the cure worse than the malady."[269]

Once Napoleon conquered Germany, he used the draft to conscript German peasants to serve in his army. In 1812 Napoleon decided to invade Russia. The Russians avoided confrontation and let the weather and long supply lines weaken the French. The French were decimated, and they retreated to Germany in 1813, where the allies ganged up on Napoleon at Leipzig. Napoleon was outnumbered and outgunned, and he withdrew. This was the beginning of the "war of national liberation" for the German people. Within two years, Napoleon was vanquished at Waterloo. The German states were on their own once more.

Perils

The period from 1650 to 1850 presented its own unique palette of perils: freezing to death, dividing up a farm to multiple heirs with the result that none of them could survive on their small farm plots, weather patterns of the "Little Ice Age" that ruined harvests, deadly accidents from the newly arrived Industrial Revolution, religious persecutions, witchcraft trials, and being forced to serve in an army. Nevertheless, this age brought some relief from the perils of 1450 to 1650. Violence and homicide rates dropped dramatically. The death toll from wars declined sharply. And the recurring plagues diminished.

Let's start with freezing to death. We all know about the famous Ice Age that blanketed much of our planet with deep ice and snow from 2.6 million years ago until it ended in about 9700 BCE. What is less well known is the "Little Ice Age" that descended over the earth from 1645 to 1715. This little ice age set the stage for some horrifically cold winters in northern Europe in which people literally froze to death in their own homes. The freezing weather forced peasants to spend up to 10 percent of their income on fuel—firewood or coal. Sometimes even that was not sufficient. The fire was too small or the fire died out in the middle of the night, and the house turned into a freezer. The death toll in Scandinavia was as high as 10 percent of the population dying from the cold. Throughout the German lands, during those seventy years, thousands of people froze to death—many in their own homes.

Another peril of this age was the traditional problem of how to divide up a farm in a just and fair way when a peasant couple had multiple children. It is estimated that in 80 percent of the German lands, the farms by tradition were handed down through "impartible inheritance." This means that the entire estate was bequeathed to one heir—usually the oldest son. The obvious advantage was that it allowed the couple to hand down a farm that was large enough for the next family to support itself. However, there were regions of Germany in which the tradition was subject to "partible inheritance," in which the farm was divided up among multiple children. The inevitable result was that the divided farms were too small to support a family. In the days when birth control was both illegal and unavailable, a common peril was the arrival of a third or fourth child. The prosperous thirty-two-acre farm would be divided into four marginal farms of eight acres each, and a generation later, those might evolve into eight farms of four acres each, and each of those farmers faced a lifetime struggle against pauperism.

Bad weather was an additional problem during this time. We have many accounts of the dreadful years of 1770 and 1771. There were heavy rains during those two consecutive years, particularly in Saxony. The crops failed. Infants and older people were usually the first to die, and then everyone was vulnerable. There were thirty-six thousand fewer births, sixty thousand more deaths, and the population of the area declined by 6 percent.[270]

One hundred years later, the year 1816 would be described as the "year without a summer."[271] There was a cold winter, and spring came late, then it rained, and the fall freeze came early. Thousands of peasants simply gave up. By June of 1817, thirty thousand people crowded into Dutch ports waiting for passage to America.

The full effect of the Industrial Revolution finally reached the German lands in 1850, and along with its blessings, it introduced new dangers. For example, as the technology of steam power was being perfected, the steam boilers were vulnerable to devastating explosions. We know that steamboats plying the Mississippi were often destroyed in a single sudden explosion. There must have been similar accidents all over the German lands as workers coped with the new power of steam, the extreme heat of blazing coal fires, and powerful machinery.

Religious persecutions were so common that they were not even recognized as "persecutions" but rather forced migrations. This was an uneasy moment in history in which there was a profusion of religious beliefs alongside a rigid intolerance of different doctrines. For example, in the dead of winter 1732–1733, twenty thousand Protestants were banished from the Roman Catholic region of Salzburg (present-day Austria). Most moved to Prussia, but eighty families emigrated to the United States to set up a Protestant settlement in present-day Georgia.

A final peril of this era was the very real risk that one would be drafted into the army to risk one's life in a war that had been sparked by the whim or greed of the prince of the kingdom. Thirty thousand men were conscripted into the German armies and then sold to the king of England for seven million British pounds. Fully twelve thousand of these soldiers were sold by Prince Friedrich II of Hesse-Cassel in January of 1776, so all the soldiers were referred to as "Hessians." They were forced to fight as mercenaries against the Americans in the Revolutionary War of 1776–1783. Those soldiers were not fighting for a patriotic cause.

They were not fighting to defend their own homeland. They were forced into fighting so that their respective princes could enjoy a substantial payment from the English king. The risk of conscription became more widespread with the militarization of Prussia in the 1800s. A hundred years later, between 1871 and 1885, a total of one and a half million Germans would leave Germany, and 95 percent came to America. A key motivation during these fourteen years was the desire to avoid three years of service in the emperor's army.

Worries

The causes for worries evolved from the previous period of 1450–1650. Some worries subsided. These years eroded the peasants' belief in heaven, hell and purgatory. Each Protestant group (Lutherans, Calvinists, Anabaptists, Pietists and others) unanimously denied the existence of purgatory, and even the Roman Catholics became skeptical about its existence. Purgatory and hell no longer paralyzed a peasant with fear.

Peasants were no longer obsessed with death. They saw death all around them, and it became familiar. If peasants were devout believers, they probably concluded that they were excellent candidates for heaven. They worried about getting children baptized as quickly as possible after birth. They certainly worried about the fate of a baby that was stillborn— for whom baptism was already too late.

There was a sharp downturn in violence beginning around 1720, which caused a big decline in violent attacks and homicides. That must have been comforting to the young German men of that day who now worried less about getting murdered.

It seems that the German peasants lived very close to the tangible events of each day. They didn't indulge in much abstract speculation. To that extent, they did not "borrow trouble" by worrying about possible problems lying in the future. It is reported that around 1700, "the threat of starvation began to fade."[272] This is partly the result of the improved agricultural techniques.

It doesn't seem that the peasants looked far ahead and worried about the long-term risks of bad weather. Peasants were also philosophical about contracting various diseases.

So, we see many worries fading. So what did the peasants worry about? First, they must have worried about becoming a pauper. The farm sizes had been declining, and the number of peasants without any land was rising. This meant that the number of paupers, beggars and prostitutes was also rising. Surely some peasants worried about sinking to the bottom of the economic ladder. Second, they worried about their religious freedom. By 1650 it was established that you should follow the religious preference of the ruler of the kingdom where you lived. But what happened if the ruler "converted" to a different religious affiliation. This might put you in jeopardy. You might have to convert or move to a different part of Germany or even emigrate to the United States. When the Prussian rulers decided to merge Calvinism with the Lutheran Church, many staunch Lutherans objected and moved to the United States. Third, the young men worried about being conscripted into the army of their prince and sent off to risk their lives fighting his petty wars.

Self-image

As we have seen in this period, there was a great divergence of social classes among those who were not of the nobility. By 1650, some very prosperous persons were able to purchase the estates of bankrupt nobility, and there was about 20 percent who were destitute, virtually penniless. The monolithic peasant culture of 476–955 had been shattered and reconstituted into multiple layers of social classes.

Prior to 1850, there was no significant improvement in the overall standard of living, but there were prosperous families. There were successful merchants and craftsmen. These families had servants themselves. At the other end of the social and economic spectrum were the beggars and the homeless.

This wide diversity of social class created a correspondingly wide range of self-images. Let us start with the poorest peasants. Historian Jerome Blum paints the following picture: "By the 1700s . . . the free peasantry made up a small fraction of the rural population of western Germany, and despite their free status, most of them had to pay dues and fees to seigniors who had established authority over them. . . . In general, the status of the peasantry worsened as one moved eastward across the continent, and it reached its nadir in the lands that lay on the other side of the Elbe River. . . . In Mecklenburg where peasants probably suffered worse treatment than anywhere else in Germany, there was an active and open trade in serfs from the mid-1600s on, though it did not receive official sanction from the government until 1757." We read in the section on New Developments that the Age of Absolutism ran from 1550 to 1800. This was the high water mark for the extreme degradation of the powerless. Poor peasants might have been more vulnerable and less respected than they had been in the Iron Age or throughout the Middle Ages.

Blum goes on to report, "The peasant was considered some lesser and sub-human form of life—a hybrid between animal and human was the way a Bavarian official put it in 1737. . . . 'I am only a serf,' the peasant would reply when asked to identify himself. They seemed without pride or self-respect, dirty, lazy, crafty and always suspicious of their masters and of the world that lay outside their village." In 1806 Germany's leading agriculturist wrote that "the evil lies deep in the present system under which the peasant becomes ever poorer, lazier and more stupid. . . . In their hopelessness, their desperation and perhaps their self-hate, peasants everywhere, man and women and often children, drank heavily and even passionately."[273] If we focus on this group of peasants, we can imagine their self-image filled with hopelessness, helplessness and despair.

We read that after 1650 both the nobility and the small emerging middle class were eager to establish social distinctions to differentiate themselves from the typical poor peasant. This differentiation took the form of detailed sumptuary laws, which dictated what those in a half-dozen different social classes could wear and what they could not wear. The whole point seems to have been to make it clear to the world that the nobles were elevated.

Ray Stannard Baker describes nineteenth-century German culture as follows: "There is the fine art of bowing. In Germany, you lift your hat to men as well as to women. If you meet General Schmoller, you raise your hat high and bring it down to your knees with a full sweep of the arm; if you meet Herr Schmidt, who is your social equal, you tip your hat as much as he does his—and no more; whereas, if you meet your tailor you respond to his low bow by the merest touch of recognition. To the initiated, every man proclaims his social position at every step by his bowing."[274] In this scenario, it must have been exhausting and demeaning for someone like the tailor who is at the bottom of the social ladder. He ventures out into the street and finds it necessary to bow and scrape to almost everyone he meets. This daily humiliation must have permeated many a mindset.

Contrast this state of mind with someone who recently migrated to the United States and writes home to his family. "I now have 100 acres of land by a paper, and it is all mine. When I am plowing, I can shut my eyes and smell the dear land under me and say it is mine, mine, mine. No one can take it away."

Although the fruits of the Industrial Revolution began to trickle into German life in the 1820s, the typical town was dominated by a few wealthy burghers. Sharp distinctions of social caste were to last in Germany right up to the era of industrialization in the 1800s.[275]

Let us balance this treatment of self-image by remembering two groups of people during this early modern era. The first group is comprised of those who were able to rise into the respectable ranks of society through their skills, hard work and good fortune. They were the few who had witnessed life getting better compared to their grandparents and parents. They must have enjoyed a sense of self-esteem and pride in their ability to provide a better life for their families. But the second group encompassed those who remained poor and continued to labor at subsistence farming. They were no better off than their peers in their small village, but importantly they were not worse off. This second group of people had the capacity to be nourished by the love and respect of their family and friends, to find meaning in productive work, to host small parties, for friends and family celebrations, to sing and dance, to enjoy a loving marriage and healthy children, to be at peace in their religion, and to live without regrets and recriminations. We can imagine that their self-image was healthy and happy.

Despite their poverty, many German peasants found jvoy and fulfillment in life, such as this happy couple dancing to the music.

Religion and values

In many ways, the religious life of the German peasants was little changed after 1650. The church still had a strong influence over the daily lives of its members. For instance, the custom of saying a prayer of thanks before a meal had become quite common in the German lands.

The church also continued to establish and enforce harsh rules. The authority of the church remained very strong in some parts of the German lands. For example, in 1662, a poor man earned his meager living by mending shoes. A man came to him on Saturday and asked the cobbler to mend his shoes in time for Sunday services. The cobbler worked on the shoes that night, and when midnight arrived, he wasn't quite finished. So, he went to bed and arose early on Sunday morning and worked privately in his own room to finish the shoes. A neighbor saw him and informed the church authorities of his working on the Sabbath. The cobbler was sent to prison.

The major change in religious life was the emergence of c, the Mennonites and the Amish. These were Anabaptist sects whose original roots were in Switzerland. Quite early in his ministry, some of Ulrich Zwingli's followers argued that Zwingli's reforms had not gone quite far enough. Hence they were called the "radical reformers." This group split from Zwingli as early as 1525, and they were soon called "the Swiss Brethren."

In general, this group emphasized "sola scriptura" (the only authority for Christian teaching is the Bible). Accordingly, because Jesus practiced foot-washing, they introduced this as part of their practice. Because the New Testament reported only adult baptisms, they strongly believed that baptism should be withheld until a person is an adult—old enough to make a responsible commitment to Jesus Christ. They were also influenced by the reports of the early Christianity community separating itself from secular society. They placed great emphasis on the admonition in Romans 12:2 "be not conformed to the world." This inspired them to maintain their humble traditions, including homemade clothes, instead of adapting to changing fashions in clothing.

The Swiss Brethren grew slowly, and by the 1600s, they were called Mennonites. By the late 1600s, they had spread from Switzerland into France, Germany and the Netherlands. Then in 1693, there was a disagreement about how to deal with people in the church who did not conform. Both parties agreed that those who lie or otherwise fail to follow the behavior code of the church should be excommunicated on a vote of the church members. This simply meant they were forbidden to participate in communion at church until they had repented. A bishop named Hans Reist taught that these persons should not be ostracized by their own families. Exclusion from communion was sufficient punishment.

However, another leader, Jacob Amman, taught that they should be totally shunned. Their family should ostracize them, forbid them to eat at the family table and cease speaking to them. In 1710 (about fifteen years after the original split), the opponents of Jacob Amman coined a term of disgrace, calling his followers "Amish." The term stuck. The rift deepened, and now there were two distinct groups—the Mennonites and the more radical Amish.

The distinction is very much alive today in the United States. Beginning in 1760, both Mennonites and Amish began emigrating to the United States to escape religious persecution from Catholics and mainstream Protestants alike. They first settled in Pennsylvania. The "Quaker State" was famous for its religious toleration. What is remarkable is that both of these groups have thrived and grown in the United States.

Today in the twenty-first century, both groups continue to dress much like their ancestors, who were German peasant farmers in the 1600s and 1700s. The Amish are more distinctive because they generally avoid mechanized travel. They also avoid electricity and telephones.

The behavior code (or "*Ordnung*") provides detailed directions for their daily behavior. They live together in rural communities. They strive to separate themselves from secular society ("be not of the world"). This separation from society has enabled them to perpetuate the original German dialects spoken in the German lands in the 1700s. It is sometimes called "Pennsylvania Dutch."

The Amish focus on humility and cooperation as opposed to individualism. They emphasize hard work and mutual support. They usually avoid insurance of any kind, and they do not participate in Social Security in the United States. They produce almost all the food that they eat. They buy very few groceries—usually limited to flour and sugar in the stores. They do not build church buildings but rather they worship every other Sunday at the home or barn of one of their members.

Their children attend one-room schools to the age of fourteen. Here they are instructed in high German. They usually do not seek further education because this could lead to social segregation and the risk of unraveling the community. The children are eligible for baptism at the age of seventeen, after which they become members of the church. The Amish are staunch pacifist and refuse military service of any kind.

Today in the United States, they are reminders of the rural lifestyle of our German ancestors from the 1600s and 1700s. In villages and small towns throughout the German lands, it was likely that the church was the most important institution in the community. Everyone was taxed for the church—whether the village had a Catholic church or a Protestant church, and most people attended. It is likely that the church provided the most important social encounter of the week.

This family is saying "grace" before the midday meal.

Reformed families in Holland and elsewhere limited the family size through birth control measures.

Family planning and birth control started early in Calvinist populations, and by the 1600s, families of two or three children were no longer a rarity. Before the Reformation, families often had six or eight children, as was still the case in Catholic Europe. The smaller family is reflected in Dutch paintings of the period. In Catholic countries, many believed that children were born as God willed, and this was pleasing to the state since it was believed at the time that the state's most precious treasure was a large population.[276]

Laws and political institutions

Let's begin by summarizing some key facts about the status of a serf in the German lands between 1650 and 1850. Serfdom had not been completely extinguished.

1. Free and unfree were relative terms. Even those who owned farmland outright still had obligations to the local lord.
2. Serfs were not slaves. They could not be killed, mutilated, sold off or separated from their families. (The only legal way to sell a serf was to sell the manor, in which case all the serfs of the manor were included in the sale.)[277] Despite this tradition, there was an active and open trade in serfs in Mecklenburg from about 1650 to about 1750. There are anecdotal reports of a lord in Schleswig-Holstein who exchanged a serf for two dogs and of other serf-owners who used their serfs as stakes in gambling at cards.[278]
3. In many cases, a serf was better off than a free person who had no financial security and possibly no land to work.
4. Within a village, a serf could enjoy considerable freedom, relative wealth and prestige. There was no direct correlation between an individual's social status and his personal freedom.

The official death knell for serfdom came with the establishment of the Napoleonic Code between 1800 and 1810. However, even after this event, it took decades for peasants to free themselves of the maze of obligations to the local lord.

Before 1800 the local lord could arbitrarily announce new local laws. Here are some actual examples from this time period: All villagers are directed to attend church every Sunday. No one may work on Sunday. The lord may dismiss any villager serving as mayor or a member of the town council. Each citizen pledges to notify the authorities when he becomes aware of an infringement of any of the village ordinances. No one may begin the harvest until the local lord's servant has removed the tithe from the fields.[279]

The villagers were not entirely powerless. If a rule was new and a sharp departure from the traditional and customary rules, this could trigger opposition or even a potential rebellion if it created a hardship. The major grievance of the villagers usually had something to do with unpaid labor—the *"Fron."* The lord might require them to support community public works projects such as hand labor, carting labor, message-carrying, hunting services such as beating the game into the open, and fishing labor as well as traditional field labor.[280]

In one case, the villagers protested several new local ordinances. They brought their concerns to the villager who was serving as mayor. He rebuffed their appeal, so they took their cause to the village court, and this time they won the support of the members of that court (who were fellow burgers). Next, they took their complaint to the bailiff. They explained that they were prepared to rebel if the lord did not make concessions. The villagers explained their willingness to make some compromises, but they insisted they would not accept a flat NO. In fact, they sent the message to the lord warning that 1. They would refuse to perform the *Fron.* (In effect, they would stage a sit-down strike.) 2. Despite their vow of personal allegiance that each swore to the lord of the manor, they were prepared to take their grievance to the imperial court.

The lord was angry at this revolt, and he briefly considered terminating the leases and expelling all families that were part of the protest. But he thought better of this action. He didn't want to create an angry, sullen populace that would find ways to sabotage his actions and his income. He agreed to a series of concessions.[281] What we learn from this specific case is that the local lord's power and authority were less secure than we sometimes suppose. His power rested to a degree on the consent of the villagers. There was a balance of reciprocity.

The *Fron* labor would survive in many villages until as late as 1850.[282] The local lord set the *Fron* requirements based on his own judgment of a family's resources. Villagers despised the *Fron*, and for this reason, the service they performed was grudging and lackluster. They worked as slowly as possible.

It was considered a privilege to be a citizen ("burger") of a village. Outsiders who wished to live in a city or village were required to apply and show financial solvency. Some would be granted "burger status," but some would be turned down. They might be granted only temporary permission to stay as "inhabitants." This meant they were always subject to expulsion for financial or other reasons. Jewish families were typically "inhabitants" and would never be granted burger status. They lived in a city or village at the sufferance of the local lord and were subject to paying a fee. Finally, burger status could not be transferred from one place to another, so it had the effect of locking most individuals into their places of birth.[283]

The pressure of too many people and not enough land caused most villages and their lords to enact ordinances that ensured that they would not be overwhelmed by beggars, the homeless, and "foreigners," whom they defined as "anyone not from the home village." Cities and villages had an obligation to support their own legal citizens if they became destitute, but they were determined not to assume responsibility for those from any other towns. Here is one real-life example from a typical village in 1763.

1. Anyone who wishes to move to the village must have the approval of the village council, swear that he is not the serf of another lord, must show that he possessed at least one thousand florins and must pay an entry fee of four florins and take the burger oath.
2. No one other than a Lutheran will be accepted as a citizen unless they get the express permission of the town council and the lord of that particular kingdom.
3. Foreign women who wish to marry a local citizen must receive permission from the local town council and the lord and, if approved, must pay a fee of two florins.
4. Anyone who owns or inherits property in the village and wishes to sell must first offer it to a legal citizen of the village. The town council has the right to approve or reject any potential foreign buyer.
5. Neither residents nor the tavern keeper may lodge a foreigner especially disreputable peddlers or tinkers, without the advance permission of the mayor of the town.[284]

Between 1650 and 1850, broad changes swept through most of the German lands, which brought temporary changes in local laws and their enforcement. For instance, the French Revolution of 1789 caused a backlash in the German lands. Fearful German rulers sought to tighten their control of the German peasants by curtailing civil rights. Then in the early 1800s, when Napoleon and his army occupied the German lands and introduced the Napoleonic Code, this was a time of liberalization—ending serfdom and introducing suffrage (the right to vote). But when Germany was liberated in 1813, the German rulers were quick to reinstitute the lords' rights over peasants, including the hated *Fron* obligations. The Revolution of 1848 very briefly brought hopes for much greater freedom and opportunity for the peasants, but when the "revolution" petered out in Germany, the rulers again were quick to suppress dissent and forced the peasants back into their subordinate roles.

Crime and punishment

Between 1650 and 1960, violence was truly tamed in Europe. There are many reasons for this. First, the end of the Thirty Years' War in 1648 brought a revulsion against violence on the part of the rulers and the peasants alike. The people were disarmed. The rulers in many kingdoms required their subjects to turn in all weapons. The rulers exerted their power over life and death. The Enlightenment is credited with changing popular mindsets to affirm cooperation and civility and abandon brutality. Rather suddenly, the homicide rate in the German lands and throughout Europe plummeted from about one hundred homicides per one hundred thousand inhabitants in the 1200s to only ten per one hundred thousand in 1650. It was a very dramatic drop.[285]

Punishments became less brutal and less public. The spectacle of public executions slowly died away. The last public hanging took place in Vienna in 1868 with all the usual attendant merrymaking.[286] Death sentences practically disappeared in Prussia around 1830.[287]

Young men continued to fight to establish their manliness, but now these fights did not permit weapons. Instead, they became bare-knuckle boxing matches.

Although homicide rates were falling dramatically in the 1600s, in the 1700s, we see a rise in severe punishments for theft. Theft of property (even when the victim did not suffer bodily injury) often resulted in executions or life in prison. Perhaps this was the result of the Industrial Revolution with its emphasis on capitalism and accumulating wealth. For example, between 1708 and 1710, one European community condemned seventy criminals to death; fifty-nine of them were punished for theft. In half of these cases, the theft was of food products, livestock or clothing without the use of violence.[288]

As in the previous period, beggars were not always objects of charity. Sometimes they morphed into real threats. Vagrants and mendicants continued to create serious social problems. Thousands of them poured into the cities, where alms were easier to come by and where perhaps there were more favorable opportunities for pilferage.[289] They robbed travelers, plundered villages and spread disease. Peasants, cowed by the threat of brigands to burn their villages, set fire to their crops or kill their animals, gave robber bands whatever they demanded. A report from 1787 asserted that the "alms" given by German villagers to beggars sometimes equaled the amounts the peasants spent on their own families.

In hindsight, crime and punishment in Germany today is radically different from how it was in Germany in 1850. We noted that the homicide rate has fallen from about 10 per 100,000 residents to only 0.85 in Germany today. Modern-day Germany has a merciful judicial system. The death penalty has been abandoned, and punishments for various crimes range from fines to imprisonment. The incarceration rate in Germany today is a modest 0.78 persons per 100,000 inhabitants versus the United States, which has the world's highest incarceration rate of 666 per 100,000 inhabitants.

Both Germany and the United States now have sizable police populations, with Germany having 296 police officers per 100,000 German residents versus a similar number of 284 in the United States. The police presence is much higher in cities than in small towns. It is the duty of the police to arrest perpetrators and then carefully investigate crimes and gather evidence to be used at trial.

Today in Germany and the United States, accusations and trials proceed very deliberately following the rule of law, which is supposed to be exactly the same regardless of wealth or political position. A fair trial is one of the highest values of modern democracy, and there are advocates such as public defenders and the American Civil Liberties Union whose mission is to ensure fair trials.

The civilized world is radically less violent than the Germany of 1560–1850. The punishments have also changed radically. Torture is expressly illegal. Accused persons are guaranteed certain rights. Punishments are not intended to cause pain. Capital punishment has become quite rare—outlawed in Germany and becoming rare in the United States. The principal punishment is incarceration. Finally, we live in diverse societies today. There is a separation of church and state. Sin in the eyes of the church is not necessarily considered a crime in the eyes of the secular state in either Germany or the United States.

Finally, the crimes people fall victim to today are often not violent crimes but rather "white-collar crimes" such as identity theft, computer hacking, and a scam where a victim is fraudulently deceived into losing money.

Language and literacy

In 1450 there were no patent laws to protect intellectual property. Gutenberg's press was simply imitated throughout Europe. The profusion of books continued. Until the 1700s, Latin maintained its stronghold on the written word. As late as 1675, about half of all books printed in Europe were printed in Latin. By 1775 a mere 5 percent were written in Latin.[290] There was a veritable explosion in the production of newspapers, magazines and periodicals of all sorts. Many were specifically directed towards or read by people previously excluded from literate discussion: women and younger girls now found a developing literature, as did the bourgeoisie.

Historian Mary Fulbrook goes on to report, "In the sphere of education, the spread of compulsory basic schooling of the 1700s . . . was supplemented by the introduction of the elite secondary schools—

Gymnasia—across Prussia. The Prussian education system was to produce major achievements in the course of the nineteenth century ranging from advances at the forefront of research to the efficient training of one of the best-educated workforces in industrialized Europe."[291]

Because there remained many people who could not read, a fixture in many communities was the town crier. He walked to the market square, rang his bell to get attention, and then read some breaking news to the assembled. It might be an announcement from the lord, or it might be general news.

In the 1700s, the German lands were "a political backwater, but it was one in which important cultural currents were flowing."[292] The German lands produced great music (Bach, Hayden, Mozart and Beethoven), great literature (Goethe and Schiller) and important philosophical thinkers (Kant and Hegel). In the late 1700s in Berlin, there appeared "salons" frequently run by women, many of them Jewish, to discuss arts, politics and ideas.

The masters mentioned above probably had little immediate impact on the peasant class, but there were also breakthroughs in popular literature in the early 1800s. Jacob and Wilhelm Grimm began collecting German folk tales during the French occupation of the German lands. They were inspired by the movement of Romanticism with its celebration of simplicity, emotion and delving into the medieval culture of Germany. The two brothers did their collecting of folk tales in a systematic, academic fashion. This was their personal "intellectual resistance" against the French occupation. They sought out storytellers who retold traditional stories that had been handed down and embellished from generation to generation. The Grimm brothers wanted to celebrate what was distinctively German. They published their first edition in 1812, and this collection included "Hansel and Gretel" and "Sleeping Beauty." The brothers were scholars, and they were preserving German culture. The stories certainly reflect German culture reaching back to medieval times. A persistent theme was the ever-present dark forest which represented danger.

There were many stories of wicked stepmothers—reflecting a common family situation because so many biological mothers died in childbirth. The stories also show the role of spinning in peasant lives. Spinning flax thread was a common communal activity performed by women working together in a *Spinnstube* ("spinning room"), where they probably kept the oral traditions alive by telling stories as they engaged in tedious work. These stories were originally filled with violence and sexuality. They were not intended for children and were initially criticized as unsuitable for young children. In fact, *Grimm's Fairy Tales* did not sell well at first. But the brothers continued to revise the stories. They gave them more detail, wove in German myths and Christian themes, and sanitized some of the violence (details of people eating children), and by the 1870s, the stories began to sell well and were finally used as children's stories.

Grimm's Fairy Tales **became a popular book in the early 1800s with dramatic stories such as "Hansel and Gretel" and "The Pied Piper of Hamelin."**

Literary trends were moving in different directions. The 1700s has been called the "century of the letter." People began to keep diaries where they put intimate thoughts and feelings on paper. This was also the period when dictionaries and grammar books appeared.[293] Another trend of the 1700s was secularization. In 1700 the Leipzig Book Fair catalog listed about 1,000 titles, half of which were on theological subjects. In 1780 the same catalog showed an increase to 2,600 titles but a decline in the percentage dealing with theology.[294]

Newspapers and magazines became popular in the 1700s. In the 1770s, more than 7,800 periodicals were being published in German versus only 58 in 1700. But strangely, university enrollment stagnated. In 1700 there were a total of 4,200 students in German universities, but that number declined in 1780 to 3,700 students.[295] Most universities were very small. Gottingen was the leading German university with 800 students in 1787, while most other universities had between 40 and 400 students. Although Germany was progressive with its university system, this progressiveness did not extend to women. Universities did not accept women until after 1900. The first German woman to get a university degree was Anita Augspurg, who earned a law degree in 1897, but had to go to Zurich to enroll in the university. Other countries were a little more accepting of female students, including Italy, which granted its first degree to a woman in 1237.

German literature was enriched in the 1700s by foreign books. *Robinson Crusoe* was translated and published in the German lands in 1719 and was an immediate success.[296] Overall German literacy inched upward to 31 percent in 1650 and 38 percent in 1750, although rural peasants were always below these averages.

Entertainment and simple pleasures

In the years after 1650, German forms of popular entertainment became very diverse. The historian James J. Sheehan points out, "Just as it is misleading to talk about a German society or economy in the 1700s, so we should be aware that no single German culture can be found. There was a segment of German society that was attracted to gory spectacles—such debased spectacles, accompanied by drunkenness, violence, and cruelty, which were as much a part of everyday cultural activity for these people as folksongs, storytellers, and traveling minstrels."[297]

Despite their poverty and despite the periodic degradations of beinng a lowly peasant in a class-conscious society, or perhaps because of these oppressions, the German peasants of this period werw always ready to release themselves from their inhibitions. They were eager to have a party with dancing, singing, and exchanging jokes- usually accompanied with great quantities of beer.

There was an overall decline in the spectacle of violence in this period. Many cruel exhibitions such as bear-baiting were prohibited. Public executions and witchcraft trials also became much less frequent.

Drinking in taverns was as popular as ever, and it was often combined with smoking cigars—a new form of smoking that arrived from the Caribbean in the 1790s. Cigars cost about three cents each, so they were mostly reserved for the prosperous.[298]

Pipe smoking began in the 1600s, to be superseded by cigar smoking in the 1800s, followed by cigarette smoking in the 1900s.

We must remember that despite a slight uptick in prosperity for some, "most people lived close to the edge of subsistence; they had little to spend on entertainment or superfluous ornamentation. A devotional picture or two, perhaps a Bible and a few precious objects, would be the extent of most people's non-essential possessions. Those few resources that could be spared from the arduous task of staying alive were usually lavished on important milestones in private or public life." Whether it was a wedding or the celebration of a craftsman becoming a journeyman, the "neighbors joined in the celebration as observers and guests, but also as the necessary source of social approval and support."[299]

Going to the spa became popular in the 1800s with the emphasis on bathing in one of Germany's hot mineral springs. Baden-Baden is situated in southwest Germany, about seventy miles west of Stuttgart, and it is one of the oldest and most famous German spas. Their hot springs were enjoyed by the Romans in 300 BCE. In 1473 Emperor Friedrich III made a famous visit to the Baden-Baden mineral baths.[300] In the early 1800s, Germans began coming to Baden-Baden for the health benefits as well as the pleasure of relaxing and socializing. Its spring water has always been high in minerals, and the serious bathers not only soak in the water but drink it as well. The men and women traditionally bathe together in the nude.

As early as 1682, Germans were enjoying the baths at Aachen.

Although the piano was first invented in about 1700, it did not catch on quickly. People preferred the traditional harpsichord. Composers began to write for the piano, and Mozart and Beethoven began to play the piano. By 1800 it was beginning to appear in prosperous homes. They were expensive. A relatively cheap pianoforte cost $200 in 1800, which was a half year's wages for a carpenter at that time. One anecdote depicts the first impression of a piano, "It is impossible to exaggerate the sensation that was produced in the village when that instrument was first heard. It was a clear, moonlit evening in summer and the windows were open. Passers-by lingered in the street. The pianoforte's range of tones and harmonies deeply impressed the new hearers, who were used to the sound of country fiddles, militia fifes and drums, and twanging mouth harps."[301] Young ladies of prosperous families were encouraged to learn to play the piano.

In 1844 the first zoo appeared in Germany (the ninth zoo in the entire world). It was established in the Tiergarten of Berlin by Frederick William IV, the King of Prussia. People were encouraged to go to the zoological gardens, where animals were treated in a supposedly civilized manner and displayed for educational purposes. It was another new refined form of entertainment.[302]

"Between 1800 and 1850, many Germans were fascinated by the performing arts."[303] Some of these performing arts were aimed directly at the audience of illiterate peasants. A perfect example is Mozart's opera *The Magic Flute*, written in German and debuted in 1791. It delighted audiences regardless of their education or sophistication.

A scene from a contemporary performance of *The Magic Flute.*

Finally, in the early 1800s, we see the first evidence of the pleasures of traveling and sightseeing. In 1828 a book publisher in Koblenz by the name of Karl Baedeker bought the rights to *Rhinereise von Mainz bis Koln: Handbuch for Schnellreisende* (*A Rhine River trip from Mainz to Cologne: A Handbook for a Quick Trip*). He edited and published this book, and it was so successful that he commissioned a series of similar books. Soon there were "Baedekers" for Belgium, Holland, the German states and Austria.[304] Sightseeing had become a new pleasure for those who could afford it.

Standard of living

After centuries of little or no improvement in the standard of living, we finally begin to see the first green shoots of improvement after 1650. Five leading economists give slightly different dates for this take-off. Max Roser points to 1650 as the beginning of a sharp rise in the standard of living, Voigtlander and Voth say it started in 1700, Beinhocker says 1750, Allen names 1815, and Angus Maddison says it did not begin in earnest until 1820. Nevertheless, all agree that a sharp upturn took place. They all call this upturn the "Great Divergence" when living standards in Europe rose much faster than in Asia or Africa. Most give credit to the Industrial Revolution.

In the 1700s, several currents of change contributed to a slightly higher standard of living.[305] They were:

1. Commerce expanded and became a source of new wealth. It might have been a German merchant who imported cloth from Belgium and England and sold it to German housewives. This merchant became part of the incipient middle class, and now he had money to spend in his local community.
2. From 1750 to 1850, there was an agrarian revolution fueled by using nitrogen-rich fertilizers to produce more food.
3. There were revolutions in transportation, communication, urbanization and literacy, which generated a higher standard of living for almost everyone, including the peasants.[306]

4. Increased urbanization was a coincident indicator of increasing prosperity. Urbanization and prosperity seemed to reinforce each other.
5. "Division of labor" was an important contributor to increased productivity.

We can visualize this when we think about the work of a full-time shoemaker who replaced the part-time work of a mother or father. Before the shoemaker, the father or mother saved the hide of a slaughtered cow, then scraped the hide to remove all the hair. Next, they tanned the hide to make it pliable leather. Then they borrowed the basic leather working tools and slowly fashioned a simple pair of leather shoes for a child in the family. This was part-time work, and the person worked slowly—learning as they made a pair of shoes for the first time.

The work was much more efficient when a full-time shoemaker bought the finished leather, used his own tools and created a dozen pairs of shoes. He cut the outline of the bottom of the shoe for each of the twelve pairs of shoes, next he cut to shape and size the "upper" of the shoe and so on. The full-time shoemaker could produce shoes much more efficiently than a typical mother or father who fashioned their first pair of homemade shoes. This division of labor (espoused by Adam Smith in his 1776 *Wealth of Nations*) greatly increased productivity. The resulting shoes were of higher quality and cost less to make. Adam Smith promoted the efficiencies of a division of labor.

Another example contrasts the charcoal maker working alone in the forest. He selects the type of wood, such as oak, and then gathers branches of approximately the same diameter. Then he inserts a stake into the ground and begins laying the oak sticks in a triangular pattern until it is about five feet tall. He cuts sod and places this around the sticks like an earthen igloo. Then, he lights the sticks on fire and lets them smolder for five or six hours. Finally, he removes the sod and harvests a fresh supply of charcoal. It is one individual working by himself and carrying out a series of different tasks.

This illustration shows how the power loom was used to manufacture cotton in 1835.

Adam Smith wrote that a division of labor was more efficient. A manufacturing task should be broken down into simple repetitive activities, and each person should do only one of those activities repetitively and pass the product on to the next worker for the next step. This created a workplace with hundreds of workers lined up side by side, each doing their single piece of work.

Of course, not all the economic news was positive. Farm holdings continued to get smaller. The growing population in Germany during this time meant that more and more peasants were left with no land. In 1550, 18 percent of the German population was comprised of cotters (who usually owned nothing more than a small cottage and a small garden) and landless peasants. By 1843 that percentage grew to 52 percent.[307] The swelling surplus of workers and diminishing supply of land meant that now there were more who could not earn their living from agriculture alone.[308] In one district in southeastern Germany, a study of land ownership in the 1780s showed that 45 percent of the families were landless or owned less than 1.8 acres, and another 39 percent owned between 1.8 and 7.2 acres.[309] The massive trend toward small farm holdings caused peasants and lords alike to adopt impartible inheritance to prevent the family farm from being split into multiple plots, each too small to provide a living.[310]

A new economic challenge appeared—indebtedness. Borrowing became more common. After a bad harvest, a poor peasant might find it necessary to borrow to put food on the table. Jerome Blum reports, "Their lords advanced them cash or produce or seed. They also borrowed from fellow peasants, who often charged them usurious rates of interest."[311] This indebtedness often condemend the borrower into becoming a life-long pauper.

Both produce and farmland begin a steep rise in value between 1730 and 1800. The inflated values tempted some nobles into excessive borrowing. Between 1760 and 1790, their burden of debt became so great that many of them lost their properties.[312] Land prices in the German lands skyrocketed between 1740 and 1800. For example, one Prussian estate that sold for 23,000 Reichstaler in 1754 was resold in 1804 for 140,000 Reichstaler.[313]

Estimated Annual per Capita Income

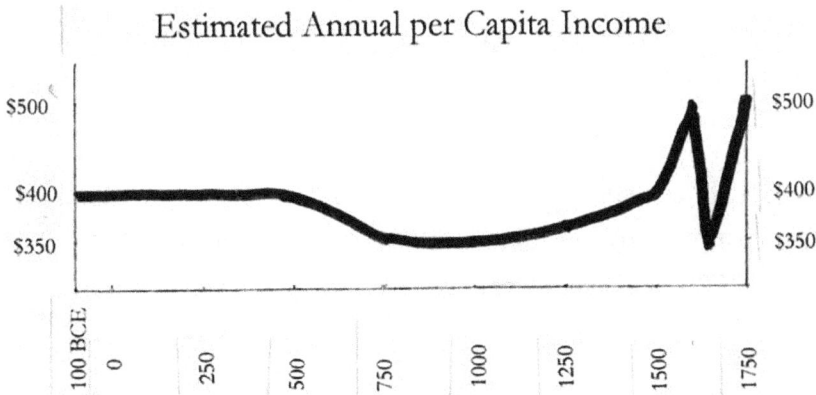

As we attempt to estimate the standard of living of the German peasant beginning in 100 BCE, we start with an estimated annual per-person income equivalent of $400 per year during the period leading up to 476. As we see in the graph above, the income varied only modestly between $350 and $500 until 1750. The big changes in the 1600s were due to the ravages of the Thirty Years' War. In the graph below, we see the beginning of a sharp rise starting in 1750. It has been reported that our ancestors who left Germany in 1850 were leaving a standard of living that was approximately that of sub-Saharan Africa today. For example, recent reports indicate that the income in Kenya today is about $1,380 per person.

In Europe as a whole, a population expansion took place between 1750 and 1850, when the population doubled.[314] In Germany, much of the population growth was rural, and the food supply of a still pre-industrial economy proved insufficient to support a growing population on the land. Food riots, rural unemployment, migration to the growing towns and even emigration across the Atlantic to America became more common.

There was an agrarian crisis from the hunger years of 1816 to 1817, followed by the depression of 1820.[315] But the Industrial Revolution was slowly penetrating the German lands and bringing an improvement in living conditions. The 1850s saw rapid economic growth in Germany; coal, iron and textile production expanded, as did the building of railways.[316]

Angus Maddison reports that the sharp rise in the standard of living began in 1820. He writes that between 1000 and 1500, per capita income almost doubled, and from 1500 to 1820, there was another increase of 56 percent. These two periods reflect very modest annual compound growth rates of 0.13 and 0.14, respectively. The year 1820 marked the turning point. Maddison calls it the moment of the Great Divergence because, in 1820, Europe enjoyed a big jump in the standard of living while China would remain stagnant for another 130 years.

Now we look back, and we know that in the next fifty years (to 1870), the per capita income in all of Europe grew by 62 percent to reach $1,960. We also know that in the next one hundred years, the per capita income mushroomed to $11,000 in 1973.

But it was too late. It so happens that the year 1820 also marked the onset of the massive migration of Germans to America. This flow of humanity would continue for the rest of the century. Although Germany had begun to improve its standard of living in 1820, many Germans were already committed to seeking a better life in America. Millions of these German peasants were now landless paupers . We have learned that from 1820 to 1870, the German standard of living rose from $1,204 to $1,960 per person (expressed in our current dollars). This places the German nineteenth-century standard of living squarely in the range of present-day Kenya at $1,380 per capita today and Sudan at $2,026 per capita today. Food remained scarce, housing was primitive, and medical care was ineffective. There was no running water and there was no hope of acquiring enough land for a prosperous farm.

From all over the German lands, the poor peasants had determined to start a new life in the new world. The great migration had begun.

A sense of time and place

During this time, everyone in the German lands had their assumptions challenged. For example, in the 1700s, the German kingdoms were very fragmented. The dialects spoken and the clothes worn in each little kingdom were all that the local people knew. "In 1765, when Goethe traveled the two hundred and fifty miles from his hometown in Frankfurt to enter the university in Leipzig, his clothes, speech and manners marked him as a foreigner. Some female companions told him he looked as if he had dropped down out of another world."[317] In 1450, virtually everyone believed that God created the world, and many thought God created everything in the year 4004 BC. (An English priest came up with this date from his understanding of the Old Testament.) But soon, this belief was challenged by the continuing discovery of fossils, which seemed to be very old. The sight of the first steam railroad train chugging across the land must have opened the imagination to new possibilities. Human beings were now able to travel at speeds that were unfathomable a few years earlier. The sound of someone playing a piano must also have been a dramatic first experience—that such combinations of sounds could exist.

Also, the French Revolution of 1789 broke the "Old Order" of things. Serfdom was abolished. The German kingdoms were conquered and occupied. This gave birth to many other possibilities. Peasant families who joined forces to spin thread from flax fibers found that their flax yarn was no longer needed. There were machines in England that were making yarn much faster and at a much lower cost. Some peasants moved to the city and created a new life for themselves where they were less vulnerable to periodic bad harvests and famines. Some peasants were actually leaving Germany and building completely new lives in the New World.

This was a period in which peasants found their perspectives changing. There were so many changes taking place that the future was destined to be quite different from their current lives.

Migrating to America

The wave of Germans migrating to America began in about 1820, and this wave turned into a surging tsunami in the ensuing one hundred years.

Why did they migrate? We have previously touched on the reasons for leaving Germany—to seek a better economic life, to avoid conscription in a German army, and to seek religious freedom.

What kind of Germans chose to migrate? It would seem that very few nobles and wealthy commoners left Germany. If they enjoyed a comfortable life, they saw little reason to turn their life upside down and say farewell to family and friends forever. At the other end of the spectrum, very few of the poorest peasants migrated. They could never afford the passage. German families saved for years to pay for the voyage, which cost about one-third of a laborer's annual wages to pay for a family of five. Another source reports that in 1850 the cost of a single ticket to cross the ocean cost two guineas (or about $51 in today's money).

The journey itself had three stages:

1. They had to travel from their hometown to the departure seaport.
2. They boarded the ship and endured the six-week voyage.
3. They usually had a final journey from the arrival seaport in the United States or Canada to their ultimate destination.

A few stayed in the port city, but the majority fanned out into the countryside.

Each of these three stages presented its own challenges. Before they ever left home, they had to accumulate the money for the passage. Then they faced the difficult choices of packing. Although a few packed a trunk, most had far less room—a single suitcase per person. They had to prioritize and include only the bare necessities—a few clothes, tools (if the family's livelihood relied on a skilled trade), a family Bible and any family heirlooms.

Getting to the departure port was a major challenge. Prior to 1870, there was only the skeleton of a railway network, so the trip of a hundred miles to the seaport was a problem. Many sailed down the Rhine River to Rotterdam. Others walked or rode in a wagon or stagecoach to the German ports of Bremen or Hamburg.

There they waited for a ship with available passenger space. Packet ships began plying the Atlantic in the 1840s on a more or less regular schedule. So, our migrants might arrive at the seaport and wait for a few days or a week for a ship to be ready to sail. While waiting, the traveler had to pass a simple physical examination to ensure that they didn't have trachoma (an infectious eye disease) or other contagious diseases that could spread on the crowded ship.

The immigrant sailing ships were surprisingly small (about one hundred and fifty feet long) and employed a small, triangular lateen sail at the stern. This is a recent photograph of a replica of the famous Jeanie Johnston.

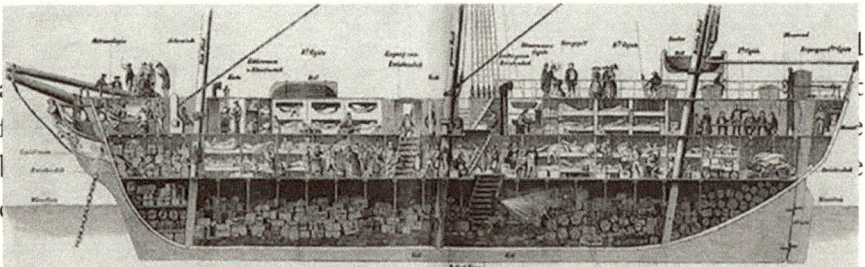

This cutaway of a migrant ship shows the lower deck just above the water line where poor migrants sailed in "steerage class."

There were three compartments between decks with the single men grouped together in the front, and couples and families in the middle with the single women at the stern—as far removed from the single men as possible. The beds were double bunks, and each bed was large—sufficient to accommodate three to five persons per bed. Most reports indicate that the mattresses were alive with fleas, lice and ticks. Each bed came with a straw mattress, but the migrants brought their own pillow, blanket and bedclothes. The sleeping compartments were equipped with chamber

192

pots and cooking equipment. In most cases, the migrants prepared their own food. The food and drink were supplied by the ship and included in the ticket price.[318]

In 1850 the weekly per person food allowance on one ship was five pounds of oatmeal, two and a half pounds of biscuits, one pound of flour, two pounds of rice, half a pound of sugar, half a pound of molasses, three quarts of water and two ounces of tea. The traveler was expected to prepare his own meals in a six-by-twelve-foot cook shop. The typical ship carried about two hundred passengers, most of them in steerage. The beds were positioned on the sides of the deck, and the middle space was devoted to a common area for eating.

The universal description of the "between decks" was that it was dark, and the air was bad. The only light was supplied by open hatchways and skylights on the deck, but during a storm, the hatchways were closed. That meant it was very dark, and if the storm continued for any length of time, the air often became frightfully bad—made worse by the stench of overflowing chamber pots and vomit. Perhaps the most common complaint was foul air and foul water. There is a reason the drinking water was often rank. As the ship sailed between America and Europe, the crew used the wooden casks to carry various liquids, from wine to vinegar to turpentine. The casks were rarely cleaned properly before being filled with drinking water. One traveler reported that the smell of the water was nauseating.

The main impression we receive is that the voyage was dirty, smelly and boring. That spells discomfort, to be sure. But what were the dangers at sea?

The obvious danger was a shipwreck or a fire on board. For example, in 1834, there were seventeen ships lost at sea and presumably sunk. Fire was another hazard; a fire on board was difficult to control. In 1848 the Ocean Monarch caught fire, and 176 people were killed. In 1858 the steamship Austria was engulfed in flames, killing an estimated five hundred passengers. The early steamships were especially vulnerable to fire because the early steam boilers were notoriously unreliable and subject to explosions. We get a larger perspective from a five-year study covering 1847 to 1852, in which forty-three emigrant ships out of 6,800 failed to reach their destination for a loss ratio of less than 1 percent.

Disease always killed more migrants than shipwrecks and sinkings. The dreaded contagious diseases were typhus, cholera, measles, diphtheria, scarlet fever, smallpox, dysentery and tuberculosis. These were especially dangerous to passengers who were malnourished. The news of a contagious disease on board was enough to "cause shipboard morale to plummet." When tuberculosis broke on the Clontarf, one passenger described the mood. "This has been a sad day, we have had five deaths, all children, the people seem to think it is a doomed ship and have lost all heart."

A more subtle health problem was seasickness. Some passengers were seasick for the entire voyage. They could not hold down food. In extreme cases, they starved to death before reaching port.

Steerage passenger mortality statistics from the 1870s[319]	
Babies under a year old	90.0 percent
Children aged 1 to 12	7.5 percent
Adults	0.35 percent

We have talked about the obvious dangers of ships being lost at sea and ravaged by a contagious disease, but there was a third problem seldom discussed—sexual assaults.

It was not uncommon for the captain of a ship to prey upon vulnerable single ladies. He would arrange to deny them food, and after they were deprived of food, he would invite a young lady to his cabin and offer her food in return for sexual favors. Sometimes he would confine her to his cabin for the rest of his voyage. Sometimes other ship's officers would similarly assault female passengers.

However, the crossing was not always miserable. In good weather, it was quite pleasant to walk on the open deck, smell the sea and enjoy the clean breezes. For some, the trip was a grand adventure. Some steerage passengers who had been used to living in the worst kind of poverty wrote that the shipboard food was the best they had ever had.

In the early 1800s, the crossing was scheduled for six weeks under sail. If the ship were becalmed or delayed by storms, the voyage could take up to fourteen weeks. Of course, in these cases, the ship would run short of provisions.

The major change came with steam power beginning in 1819 when the Savannah added supplementary steam engines to its sailing ship. From 1820 to 1850, hybrid sailing ships sometimes used steam power on calm seas or to maneuver in port. In about 1850, pure steamships appeared. These were usually larger ships carrying four to five hundred passengers. Steamships were revolutionary because they immediately shortened the crossing time from six weeks to two weeks. The passengers paid for the speed and convenience. The tickets on steamships cost twice as much as sailing ships. This meant that poor peasants continued to use sailing ships.

Sailing ships and steamships competed for business from the 1850s until 1879, when the last sailing ship set sail from Hamburg.

Upon arrival at the destination port, the passengers disembarked and stood in line for a six-second physical where a doctor looked for obvious symptoms that the traveler was not fit to enter the country. They looked for mental illness and contagious diseases. The downside of this part of the immigrant experience has been much exaggerated. In fact, over time, only 2 percent of all arrivals were declared unfit.

In the United States, we have been accustomed to thinking of immigrants seeing the Statue of Liberty and arriving at Ellis Island. But the Statue of Liberty was not completed until 1886, and Ellis Island did not become an immigration center until 1892. Prior to that, my ancestors and most immigrants landed at the southern tip of Manhattan at Castle Gardens.

Here they became oriented with their new country. They could purchase travel tickets, exchange money, learn about employment opportunities and be warned about scammers waiting for them just outside the doors. Sometimes the family spent a night or two sleeping on the floor of the immigration office until they got their bearings.

Once they left the immigration center at the seaport, the migrants began the third and final stage of the journey to their destination. In the early days, there were no railroads.

The first railway did not connect New York with Chicago until 1853. The migrants heading to the Midwest traveled on riverboats down the Ohio River as well as stagecoaches.

When rail transportation was available, it became the preferred method of travel. In any case, there must have been small towns and country farms that could only be reached by walking or riding in a horse-drawn wagon.

The vast majority of these immigrants never saw their family or homeland again. We have heard surprising reports that as many as one-third returned to their homeland, but we have no reliable statistics until 1908.

Here are the "return" statistics after 1908. Of those who came from southern Italy, 61 percent returned. The Jews were unlikely to return, and only 6 percent of the Irish went back to Ireland. It is reported that 16 percent of the Germans who came to America went back to Germany.

The vast majority stayed in the United States, and many wrote letters to friends and family with glowing descriptions of the opportunities in this new world.

Table talk: Migrating to America alone

A family is sitting down to supper at their restaurant in the small village of Hochstadten in the province of Hesse. The gathered family is Philip Seeger and his wife Anna Maria, who own the restaurant. Also at the table are their adult son Philip, their thirteen-year-old daughter Elisabeth, and their nephew Wilhelm, also aged thirteen. Anna Maria is Wilhelm's aunt. Her younger brother, Heinrich, had been a famous lithographer for the emperor in Vienna when he died suddenly of a heart attack at the tender age of thirty-nine. He left his wife, Anna Magdalena Muller, and their three children, Georg, Frieda and Wilhelm. Anna Magdalena decided to start a new life in America, and she took Georg and Frieda, her two oldest children, with her. She knew she had to earn a living in America and didn't see how she could do that and take care of all three of her children. So she asked her sister-in-law and her husband if they would take care of her youngest child, Wilhelm, until she could send for him. Uncle Philip owned the best restaurant in town, and they were doing very well. They quickly agreed. Young Wilhelm was the same age as their daughter Elisabeth, and they were happy playmates. Now it is five years later—1887. Aunt Anna Maria serves the soup and begins the conversation. She has big news.

Anna Maria: "Wilhelm, I have some wonderful news for you."

Wilhelm looks up: "What is it?"

Anna Maria held out a letter: "We just received this letter from your mother in America."

Wilhelm: "Oh, what did she say?"

Anna Maria: "She says you are about to join them in America."

Wilhelm has been waiting for this day, but now he has mixed emotions—excitement and joy, but mostly a lot of questions. He asks: "How will I get there? Who will go with me? Can Elisabeth come too? Where will we live? Where do I board a ship? Where will I arrive in America? How much does it cost?"

Uncle Philip speaks out: "Wilhelm, one question at a time, and don't worry about the cost. Your mother sent the money for your ticket. We are going to work out the details."

Wilhelm: "Well, can Elisabeth come too?"

Philip: "I'm afraid not, Wilhelm. She's our only daughter. We need her here with us. But you will be rejoining your family at last. We are very happy for you."

Wilhelm: "I'm happy too, of course. But tell me everything."

Anna Maria: "Well, the modern steamships now travel regularly between Hamburg and New York. Your mother lives in Portland, Oregon, with your sister Frieda. Your older brother Georg is living in Chicago. He works as a lithographer and married earlier this year. We understand he is doing well. So, you will settle in Portland with your mother and sister."

Wilhelm: "How will I get to Portland?"

Anna Maria: "Your mother will take you. They have regular trains running between Portland and New York. Anna Magdalena is taking a train from Portland to New York and will meet you at the immigration center at Castle Gardens. Then she will take you back to Portland with her."

Wilhelm: "Will I take one of those big sailing ships?"

Philip: "Not exactly. The sailing ships are almost gone. They were too slow for most people. They took six weeks to cross the ocean. The big new steamships take only two weeks."

Wilhelm: "But will I be all alone? I mean, it's okay, but I was just wondering."

Philip: "I don't think so. I will take you to the port. We will take a stagecoach from Hochstadten to Frankfurt and then a train from Frankfurt to Hamburg. At the ship, I will find a nice family to look after you. Perhaps a family with a boy or girl your age. I will give them some money to cover any extra costs for you. You will be allowed to stay with them in the family section of the ship. I am confident that we will find a good family to take you in and deliver you to your mother when the ship docks. I will also find the ship's captain and have a word with him to make sure you are well taken care of."

Wilhelm: "What will I eat?"

Philip laughs: "That's my boy. I like a man who is thinking about good food. We will prepare two traveling bags for you—one with your clothes and your books and one filled with your favorite foods, including our special pumpernickel bread and plenty of Black Forest ham. Of course, the ship provides three meals a day throughout your trip, but we will give you plenty of special food for yourself and to share with your adoptive family."

Wilhelm now turns to Elisabeth. She has tears in her eyes, and she finally speaks: "Wilhelm, how I will miss you!"

Selected Bibliography

Allen, Robert C. *The Great Divergence in European Wages and Prices from the Middle Ages to the First World War*. Academic Press, 2001.

Anderson, Bonnie S., and Judith P. Zinsser. *A History of Their Own*. Vol. 1. New York: Perennial Library, Harper & Row, 1988.

Armstrong, Dorsey. *The Medieval World*. Chantilly, VA: The Teaching Company, 2009.

Bainton, Roland. *The Reformation of the Sixteenth Century*. Boston: Beacon Press, 1952.

Baker, Ray Stannard. *Seen in Germany*. London: Harper & Brothers, 1902.

Barraclough, Geoffrey, ed. *The Times Atlas of World History*. London: Times Books Limited, 1978.

Barzun, Jacques. *From Dawn to Decadence: 1500 to the Present*. New York: Harper Collins Publishers, 2000.

Bates, Alfred. *The Drama: Its History, Literature and Influence on Civilization*. Vol. 10. London: Athenian Society, 1903.

Bayard, Tania, ed. and trans. *A Medieval Home Companion: Housekeeping in the Fourteenth Century*. New York, NY: Harper Collins, 1991.

Beinhocker, Eric D. *The Origin of Wealth*. Harvard Business School Press, 2006.

Bernstein, William J. *A Splendid Exchange: How Trade Shaped the World*. London: Atlantic Books, 2008.

Bloch, Marc. *Feudal Society*. Vol. 1, *The Growth and Ties of Dependence*, London: Routledge & Kegan Paul Ltd., 1961.

Blum, Jerome. *The End of the Old Order in Rural Europe*. Princeton University Press, 1978.

Braudel, Fernand. *Civilization & Capitalism: 15th–18th Century.* Vol. 1, *The Structures of Everyday Life.* University of California Press, 1981.

———. *Civilization & Capitalism: 15th–18th Century.* Vol. 2, *The Wheels of Commerce*, University of California Press, 1982.

———. *Civilization & Capitalism: 15th–18th Century.* Vol. 3, *The Perspective of the World*, Harper & Row, 1984.

Brown, Peter. *The World of Late Antiquity: AD 150–750.* New York: W. W. Norton & Company, 1971.

Bryson, Bill. *A Short History of Nearly Everything.* New York: Broadway Books, 2003.

———. *At Home.* New York: Doubleday, 2010.

Bynum, William. *The History of Medicine: A Very Short Introduction.* Oxford University Press, 2008.

Caesar, Julius. *The Gallic War.*

Cantor, Norman F. *The Civilization of the Middle Ages.* New York: HarperCollins Publishers, 1963.

Collins, Roger, E. *Early Medieval Europe 300–1000.* New York: Palgrave, 1999.

Conner, Clifford D. *A People's History of Science.* Nation Books, 2005.

Cooke, Jean, Ann Kramer, and Theodore Rowland-Entwistle. *History's Timeline: A 40,000 Year Chronology of Civilization.* Ward Lock Limited, 1981.

Cunliffe, Barry. *The Oxford Illustrated History of Prehistoric Europe.* Oxford University Press, 1994.

Daniels, Roger. *Coming to America: A History of Immigration and Ethnicity in American Life.* New York: Harper Perennial, 1990.

Dean, Trevor. *Crime in Medieval Europe.* Edinburgh: Pearson Education, 2001.

Derry, T. K. and Trevor I. Williams, *A Short History of Technology from the Earliest Times to A.D. 1900.* Oxford University Press, 1960.

Easterbrook, Gregg. *The Progress Paradox: How Life Gets Better While People Feel Worse.* Random House, 2003.

Fagan, Brian. *The Little Ice Age: How Climate Made History 1300–*

1850. New York: Basic Books, 2000.

Freese, Barbara. *Coal: A Human History*. New York: Perseus Publishing, 2003.

Fulbrook, Mary. *A Concise History of Germany*. Cambridge University Press, 1991.

Garland, Robert. *The Other Side of History: Daily Life in the Ancient World*. Chantilly, VA: The Teaching Company, 2012.

Gibbon, Edward. *The History of the Decline and Fall of the Roman Empire*. New York: The Heritage Press, 1948.

Gies, Frances and Joseph Gies. *Marriage and the Family in the Middle Ages*. Harper & Row Publishers, 1987.

———. *Life in a Medieval Village*. Harper & Row Publishers, 2000.

Gonzalez-Cruzzi, F. *A Short History of Medicine*. New York: The Modern Library, 2007.

Grant, Neil. *Everyday Life in the Eighteenth Century*. Morristown, NJ: Silver Burdett Company, 1983.

Hanawalt, Barbara A. *The Ties that Bound, Peasant Families in Medieval England*. New York: Oxford University Press, 1986.

Harrison, Molly and O. M. Royston. *How They Lived: 1485–1700*. Oxford: Basil Blackwell & Mott Ltd., 1963.

Haven, Kendall. *100 Greatest Science Discoveries of All Time*. Westport, CT: Libraries Unlimited, 2007.

Haywood, John. *Atlas of the Celtic World*. New York: Thames & Hudson, 2001.

Holmes, Urban Tigner, Jr. *Daily Living in the Twelfth Century*. Madison: University of Wisconsin Press, 1952.

Heer, Friedrich. *Milestones of History*. Vol. 2, *Fires of Faith*. Newsweek Books, 1970.

Imhof, Arthur E. *Lost Worlds: How Our European Ancestors Coped with Everyday Life and Why Life is So Hard Today*. Charlottesville, VA: University Press of Virginia, 1996.

Jenner, Greg. *A Million Years in a Day*. Thomas Dunne Books, 2015.

Jones, George F. *German-American Names*. Baltimore: Genealogical Publishing Co. Inc., 1990.

Jones, Terry and Alan Ereira. *Medieval Lives*. London: BBC Books,

2004.

Kelly, John. *The Great Mortality*. New York: HarperCollins Publishers, 2005.

Lacey, Robert and Danny Danziger. *The Year 1000, What Life was like at the Turn of the First Millennium*. Boston: Little, Brown and Company, 1999.

Langer, William L., ed. *An Encyclopedia of World History*. Boston, MA: Houghton Mifflin Company, 1940.

Larkin, Jack. *The Reshaping of Everyday Life: 1790–1840*. Harper & Row, 1988.

Lautourette, Kenneth Scott. *A History of Christianity*. New York: Harper & Brothers, 1953.

Maddison, Angus. *Growth and Interaction in the World Economy: The Roots of Modernity*. Washington, DC: The AEI Press, 2005.

Manchester, William. *A World Lit Only by Fire*. Boston, MA: Little, Brown and Company, 1992.

Middleton, Hayden. *The Sixteenth Century*. Silver Burdett Company, 1986.

Mollat, Michel. *The Poor in the Middle Ages*. Yale University Press, 1978.

Mortimer, Ian. *The Time Traveler's Guide to Medieval England: A Handbook for Visitors to the Fourteenth Century*. New York: Simon & Schuster, Inc., 2008.

Muchembled, Robert. *A History of Violence from the End of the Middle Ages to the Present*. Cambridge, UK: Polity Press, 2012.

Nees, Greg. *Germany: Unraveling an Enigma*. Boston: Intercultural Press, 2000.

Nelson, Lynn Harry. *Lectures in Medieval History*. University of Kansas.

Newman, Paul B. *Daily Life in the Middle Ages*. Jefferson, NC: McFarland and Company, Inc., 2001.

Norberg, Johan. *Progress: Ten Reasons to Look Forward to the Future*. Oneworld Publications, 2016.

O'Byrne, John, ed. *A Guide to Advanced Skywatching*. San Francisco: Fog City Press, 1997.

Orme, Nicholas. *Medieval Children*. Yale University Press, 2003.

Ozment, Steven. *When Fathers Ruled: Family Life in Reformation Europe*. Cambridge, MA: Harvard University Press, 1983.

Paston-Williams, Sara. *The Art of Dining: A History of Cooking & Eating*. The National Trust, 1993.

Picture History of the World. New York, NY: Grosset & Dunlap, 1979.

Piponnier, Francoise and Perrine Mane. *Dress in the Middle Ages*. Yale University Press, 1997.

Porter, Roy, ed. *The Cambridge Illustrated History of Medicine*. Cambridge, UK: Cambridge University Press, 1996.

Power, Eileen. *Medieval People*. Doubleday Anchor Books, 1955.

Renard, G. and G. Weulersse. *Life and Work in Modern Europe: Fifteenth to Eighteenth Century*. New York: Barnes & Noble, Inc., 1968.

Riello, Giorgio. *Cotton, the Fabric that Made the Modern World*. Cambridge University Press, 2013.

Riley, James. "Estimates of Regional and Global Life Expectancy, 1800–2001." *Population and Development Review* 31, no. 3.

Rippley, Lavern. *Of German Ways*. New York: Gramercy Publishing Company, 1986.

Rosenwein, Barbara H. *A Short History of the Middle Ages*. Peterborough, Ontario: Broadview Press, 2002.

Roser, Max. *Economic Growth*.

Rowling, Marjorie. *Life in Medieval Times*. New York, NY: Penguin Publishing, 1968.

Sanner, Burkhard. "Baden-Baden a famous Thermal Spa with a Long History." *GHC Bulletin*, September 2009.

Scheer, Teva J. *Our Daily Bread: German Village Life, 1500–1850*. North Saanich, BC: Adventis Press, 2010.

Sheehan, James J. *German History: 1770–1866*. Oxford: Oxford University Press, 1989.

Singman, Jeffrey L. *The Middle Ages: Everyday Life in Medieval Europe*. New York: Sterling Publishing, 1999.

Smith, Page. *The Rise of Industrial America: A People's History of the Post-Reconstruction Era*. New York: McGraw-Hill Book Company, 1984.

Southern, R. W. *The Making of the Middle Ages*. New Haven: Yale University Press, 1953.

Standage, Tom. *A History of the World in 6 Glasses*. New York, NY: Walker & Company, 2005.

———. *An Edible History of Humanity*. New York, NY: Walker & Company, 2009.

Sumption, Jonathan. *The Age of Pilgrimage*. Mahwah, NJ: Hidden Spring, 2003.

Tacitus. *Germania*. Cambridge, MA: Harvard University Press, 1963.

Tannahill, Reay. *Food in History*. Stein and Day Publishers, 1973.

Taylor, A. J. P. *The Course of German History*. Oxon, UK: Routledge Classics, 1945.

Todd, Malcom. *The Early Germans*. Malden, MA: Blackwell Publishing, 1992.

Totten, Christine M. *Roots in Rhineland: America's German Heritage in Three Hundred Years of Immigration, 1683–1983*. German Information Center, 1983.

Voltaire. Essay on Customs.

Watson, Malcolm W. *Theories of Human Development*. Chantilly, VA: The Teaching Company, 2002.

Weiner, Robert I. *The Long 19th Century*. Chantilly, VA: The Teaching Company, 2005.

Wells, Peter S. *The Battle that Stopped Rome*. W. W. Norton & Company, 2003.

White, Lynn, Jr. *Medieval Technology and Social Change*. Oxford University Press, 1962.

Wigelsworth, Jeffrey R. *Science and Technology in Medieval European Life*. Westport, CT: Greenwood Publishing Group Inc., 2006.

Wilson, Bee. *Consider the Fork: A History of How We Cook and Eat*. Basic Books, 2012.

Wust, Klaus and Heinz Moos. *Three Hundred Years of German Immigrants in North America: 1683–1983*. Verlags-GmjbH, 1983.

Acknowledgments

First, I am deeply indebted to two faceless sources—Google and Wikipedia. They have been particularly useful in filling out my research and also in surfacing possible public-domain images that could enhance this book.

An old friend, Doug Armato, Director of the University of Minnesota Press, gave me an invaluable referral to one of his staff experts, Kristian Tvedten, who, in turn, devoted some of his personal time to guiding me through the labyrinth of picture permissions and the art of finding images in the public domain. His help was enormous.

When I conceived of this book, it was a family project. I wrote it for my extended family, and I engaged the assistance of my immediate family. My daughter, Katrina, encouraged me to read drafts to her during a family vacation. Throughout this long process (over five years of research), my wife and former English teacher, Mary Beth, offered me her wisdom and insight.

I want to thank my copyeditor, Beth Williams, who has an eagle eye for grammar but, more importantly, has an ear for smoothing out my sometimes awkward sentences. I continually shake my head in wonder at her touches. Finally, I thank Joshua Weber, who seems to be the midwife at Calumet Editions. Josh has facilitated the birthing process with patience, good cheer and grace.

Illustration Credits

The photographs and illustrations in this book come from a variety of sources listed below. In each case I have tried to provide as much information as possible, including the name of the artist or illustrator, title of the work, date, and the museum or library where the work is held.

Part One

5 Ferdinand Pauwels, *Luther Hammers His 95 These to the Door*, 1872, oil on canvas. Eisenach, Wartburg-Stiftung Collection.

6 Pieter Brueghel the Younger, *The Payment of the Tithes*, 1617–1622, oil on panel.

8 WikiCommons.

11 Wikipedia Commons.

13 Map of "Age of Exploration" on Wikipedia adapted and simplified by the author.

15 Jost Amman, *Papiermuhle mit Wasserradantrieb*, 1568, woodcut.

19 Original drawing by the author.

20 Drawing by Michael Martorelli.

22 Photograph of the Albrecht Durer house built in 1480 in Nuremberg, Germany. Photograph by Daderot, Creative Commons CCO 1.0 Universal Public Domain Dedication.

24 Bibliotheque Nationale, Paris.

26 "Women spinning flax in the fifteenth century."

30 Pieter Brueghel the Elder, *The Harvesters*, 1565. Metropolitan Museum, New York.

31 Painting by Jean Bourdichon, ca. 1457–1521.

33 Jan Brueghel the Elder, *Visit to the Tenants*, ca. 1597, oil. Kunsthistorisches Museum, Vienna.

34 Pieter Brueghel the Elder, *Peasant Wedding* detail, 1567, oil on panel. Kunsthistorisches Museum, Vienna.

36 A handgun ca. 1700–1730. Wikipedia\flintlock.

37 Giuseppe Bertini, *Galileo Galilei Showing the Doge of Venice How to Use the Telescope*, 1858, fresco.

40 Frans Hals, *The Gipsy Girl*, 1628, oil. Louvre, Paris.

42 Woodcut from 1498, Bibliotheque Nationale, Paris.

43 Painting, Archiv fur Kunst und Geschichte, London.

45 Painting by Xavier Romero-Frias of a ship with lateen sails, Creative Commons Attribution-Share Alike 3.0.

52 Image entitled "Syphilis treatment," created between 1497 and 1498.

56 Line-art drawing from the archives of Pearson Scott Foresman, donated to the Wikimedia Foundation and released to the public domain by its author.

60 Pieter Brueghel the Elder, *The Hunters in the Snow*, 1566, oil on oak panel. Kunsthistorisches Museum, Vienna.

61 Sebastiaen Vrancx, *Soldiers Plundering a Farm during the Thirty Years' War*, 1620, oil on panel. Deutsches Historisches Museum, Berlin.

62 Jacques Callot, *The Miseries and Misfortunes of War* detail, 1633, etching, created in during the Thirty Years' War. Wikipedia.

64 Ludovico Carracci, *An Angel Frees the Souls of Purgatory*, ca.1610. Pinacoteca Vaticana.

71 Marinus van Reymerswaele, *The Tax Collector*, 1542. Alte Pinakothek, Munich.

72 Drawing by Michael Martorelli.

73 Image produced by Jan Luyken in 1685. Wikimedia Commons.

76 Original drawing by the author based on information at "Our World in Data" which references the World Bank and CIA Factbook.

78 This image is part of a page from the *Margarita Philosophica Nova*, written in 1508 by Gregor Reisch and printed by Gruninger of Strasbourg, France.

79 Herzog Anton Ulrich-Museum, Braunschweig, Germany.

81 Pieter Brueghel the Elder, *Children's Games*, 1560. Kunsthistorisches Museum, Vienna.

82 Pieter Brueghel the Elder, *Peasant Dance*, 1569. Kunsthistorisches Museum, Vienna.

82 Pieter Brueghel the Elder, *Wedding Dance*, 1566. Detroit Institute of Arts, Detroit, Michigan.

83 Pieter Brueghel the Elder, *Landscape with Skaters and Bird Trap*, 1565. Royal Museum of Fine Arts of Belgium, Brussels.

87 Louis L. Nain, *Peasant Family in an Interior*, ca. 1640, oil on canvas. Louvre, Paris.

88 Pieter Brueghel the Elder, *The Cripples*, 1568. Louvre, Paris.

Part Two

92 Bildarchiv Preussischer Kulturbesitz, Berlin.

93 Friedrich Pecht, *The Paulskirche Casinofraktion*, 1849, lithograph. Transferred to de.wikipedia. Public domain in USA.

95 From a book entitled *Die Gartenlaube,* published by Ernest Keil in Leipzig in 1871.

98 William Wyld, *Manchester from Kersal Moor*, 1852. Originally commissioned by Queen Victoria, it is now in the Royal Collection.

100 Caspar David Friedrich, *Two Men Contemplating the Moon*, ca. 1825–1830, oil on canvas. Metropolitan Museum of Art, New York City.

101 Philipp Veit, 1848, fresco originally painted on a wall in the Paulskirche in Frankfurt and now in the Germanisches Nationalmuseum in Nuremberg.

102 A cartoon published in *Harper's Weekly* showing German emigrants boarding a steamer in Hamburg in 1874. Wikipedia.

104 Dithmarscher Landesmuseum Meldorf, Schleswig-Holstein, Creative Commons, Bullenwachter (CC BY-SA 3.0).

105 Creative Commons, Daniel Schwen (CC BY-SA 4.0).

110 Creative Commons, Ceridwen (CC BY-SA 2.0 FR).

111 Auguste Renoir, *Two Young Girls at the Piano*, 1892. Musee d'Orsay, Wikimedia Commons.

115 Illustration of the rat catcher. British Library, Wikimedia Commons.

116 Drawing by Michael Martorelli.

118 *National Geographic*.

121 Plate 61 from the *Cryes of the City of London Drawne after the Life*. British Museum, Wikimedia Commons.

126 Robert C. Hinkley, *The First Operation with Ether*, ca. 1890, oil on canvas. University of Medicine Library, Harvard University, Wikimedia Commons.

127 Drawing by Michael Martorelli.

128 Andrew Ure, 1881, illustration of the Havgreaves' Spinning Jenny. Wikimedia Commons.

130 A German nineteenth century clock made by Gustav Becker. Image by Luekk (CC By-SA 3.0), Wikimedia Commons.

132 England introduced fast and inexpensive mail in 1840 featuring the young Queen Victoria on the penny stamp.

135 *Deutsches Worterbuch,* 1854. Leipzig, British Library, London.

140 Postkutsch, Creative Commons Attribution-Share Alike by-sa 3.0 license, Wikimedia Commons.

141 Carl Rakeman, *Construction of a Macadam Road*, 1823. Wikimedia Commons.

143 OpenStreetMap (CC BY-SA 2.0), Wikimedia Commons, enhanced by the author.

144 Lithograph. Wikimedia Commons.

148 Wilhelm Leibl, *Das Uncleiche Paar*, 1876–77, oil. Stadel Museum, Frankfurt am Main.

151 Reinhard Zimmerman, *Die Impfstube*, 1856. Bildarchiv Preussischer Kulturbesitz.

158 Rama (CC BY-SA 2.0 FR), Wikimedia Commons.

166 Artist unknown, *Feiernde Bauern* (*Celebrating Peasants*), eighteenth or nineteenth century.

169 Jan Steen, *Grace Before Meat*, 1626?–1679. National Gallery, London.

170 Frans Hals, *Family Portrait*, 1635, oil on canvas.

178 Arthur Rackham, 1909, illustration from *The Fairy Tales of the Brothers Grimm*, Constable & Company, London.

179 Kate Greenway, 1910, illustration from *The Pied Piper of Hamelin,* Frederick Warne and Company, London.

181 Frans Hals, *The Smoker*, ca. 1623–25, oil on panel. Metropolitan Museum of Art, Marquand Collection, Gift of Henry G. Marquand, 1889.

182 Jan Luyken, *Innenansicht des Kaiserbades in Aachen*, 1682.

183 Front page of the original edition of the libretto of Mozart's opera *Die Zauberflote* from the debut performance in Vienna, 1791.

186 T. Allom, 1835, illustration, from *History of the Cotton Manufacture in Great Britain* written by Sir Edward Baines.

187 Original drawing by the author.

188 Original drawing by the author.

192 A photograph taken by Paul Dolan from a dinghy while crossing the Atlantic Ocean of the replica of the Jeanie Johnston immigrant ship. Creative Commons Attribution-Share by-sa 3.0 license.

192 Illustration from *Die Gartenlaube Leipzig Fruft Neil*, 1854. The Smithsonian Museum of American History.

Endnotes

1   "German Peasants' war," Wikipedia, https://bit.ly/3LhIiTZ.

2   A. J. P. Taylor, *The Course of German History* (Hamish Hamilton Ltd., 1945), 8.

3   Fernand Braudel, *Civilizations and Capitalism: 15th–18th Century*, vol. 1, *The Structures of Everyday Life* (University of California Press, 1982), 397.

4   "Ink," Wikipedia, https://en.wikipedia.org/wiki/Ink.

5   T. K. Derry and Trevor I. Williams, *A Short History of Technology from the Earliest Times to A.D. 1900* (New York: Dover Publications, Inc., 1993), 236.

6   Braudel, 400.

7   "Frankfurt Book Fair," Wikipedia, https://en.wikipedia.org/wiki/Frankfurt_Book_Fair.

8   Clifford D. Conner, *A People's History of Science* (Nation Books: New York, 2005), 295.

9   Roland Bainton, *The Reformation of the Sixteenth Century* (Boston: Beacon Press, 1952), 244–245.

10 Ibid., 246.

11 Ibid., 247.

12 Ibid., 249.

13 Barbara Freese, *Coal: A Human History* (New York: Perseus Publishing, 2003), 2.

14 Ibid., 33.

15 Alan D. Dyer, "Wood and Coal: A Change of Fuel," *History Today* 26, Issue 9, September 1976, https://bit.ly/3vOvMoO.

16 Ibid.

17 Conner, 249–250.

18   Braudel, 295.

19   Ibid., 297.

20   Ibid., 301.

21   Ibid., 304.

22   Ibid., 487.

23   Jerome Blum, *The End of the Old Order in Rural Europe* (Princeton: Princeton University Press, 1978), 82.

24   James J. Sheehan, *German History, 1770–1866* (Oxford: Oxford University Press, 1989), 96.

25   Blum, 140.

26   Hayden Middleton, *The Sixteenth Century* (London: Silver Burdett Company, 1982), 54.

27   Braudel, vol. 1, 349.

28   Sheehan, 752.

29   Braudel, vol. 1, 352.

30   Middleton, 33.

31   Tannahill, 226f.

32   Middleton, 24.

33   Braudel, vol. 1, 110–111.

34   Ibid., 24.

35   Ibid., 50.

36   Standage, 111.

37   Laura Poppick, "Let Us Now Praise the Invention of the Microscope," *Smithsonian Magazine*, March 30, 2017, https://bit.ly/3kk5ANb.

38   "Invention of the Pencil," Enchanted Learning, https://bit.ly/3rV32cu.

39   Martyn Cornell, "A short history of bottled beer," Zythophile, https://bit.ly/3MCZYcX.

40   Gabriele Mentges, "European Fashion (1450–1950)," European History Online, June 3, 2011, https://bit.ly/38u9Lnd.

41   Middleton, 16.

42   Erasmus, *De civilitate morum puerilium*, https://bit.ly/3ETngZE.

43   Derry and Williams, 212.

44   Ibid., 207.

45   Braudel, vol. 1, 423.

46   Ibid., 415.

47   Ibid., 423.

48   Derry and Williams, 207.

49   Robert Muchembled, *A History of Violence from the End of the Middle*

Ages to the Present (Cambridge, UK: Polity Press, 2012), 30.

50   Gies, 303.

51   William Manchester, *A World Lit Only by Fire* (Boston: Little Brown and Company, 1992), 67.

52   Orme, 55–57.

53   Middleton, 26.

54   Porter, 35.

55   Ibid., 102.

56   Ibid., 36.

57   Ibid., 46.

58   Middleton, 15.

59   Conner, 301f.

60   Jeffrey R. Wigelsworth, *Science and Technology in Medieval European Life* (Westport, CT: Greenwood Publishing Group Inc., 2006), 107.

61   Conner, 3.

62   Ibid., 97.

63   Porter, 80.

64   Ibid.

65   Orme, 113.

66   Braudel, vol. 1, 386.

67   Wigelsworth, 94.

68   Ibid., 95.

69   Ibid.

70   Ibid., 97.

71   Ibid., 95.

72   Braudel, 395.

73   Ibid., 392.

74   Ibid., 53.

75   *Picture History of the World* (Grosset & Dunlap, 1979), 148.

76   Jacques Barzun, *From Dawn to Decadence: 1500 to the Present* (New York: Harper Collins Publishers, 2000), 231.

77   Wigelsworth, 100.

78   Ibid.

79   Braudel, vol. 1, 53.

80   Arthur E. Imhof, *Lost Worlds: How our European Ancestors Coped with Everyday Life and Why it is so Hard Today* (Charlottesville, VA: University Press of Virginia, 1996), 4.

81   Jones, 26.

82   Imhof, 91.

83   Bernstein, 144.

84   Muchembled, 35.

85   "Ignaz Semmelweis," Wikipedia, https://bit.ly/3KLfMJl.

86   Barzun, 44.

87   Imhof, xii.

88   Derry and Williams, 39.

89   Teva J. Scheer, *Our Daily Bread: German Village Life, 1500–1850* (North Saanich, BC: Adventis Press, 2010), 11f.

90   Ibid., 25.

91   Muchembled, 76.

92   Ibid., 77.

93   Ibid., 70.

94   Ibid., 122.

95   Ibid., 132.

96   Ibid., 135.

97   Ibid., 140.

98   Scheer, 28f.

99   Middleton, 39.

100   Conner, 367.

101   Fulbrook, 28.

102   "Luther Bible," Wikipedia, https://bit.ly/3MSvmnZ.

103   Fulbrook, 51.

104   Orme, 261.

105   Conner, 295.

106   Braudel, vol. 1, 400.

107   "Oberammergau," Wikipedia, https://bit.ly/3yfBWkm.

108   Alfred Bates, *The Drama: Its History, Literature and Influence on Civilization*, vol. 10, 28–32.

109   Ibid.

110   Newman, 165.

111   Braudel, vol. 1, 237.

112   Newman, 182.

113   Braudel, vol. 1, 236.

114   Ibid., 234.

115   Ibid., 261–262.

116   Derry and Williams, 39–40.

117   Fulbrook, 51.

118 Ibid., 33.

119 Robert C. Allen, *The Great Divergence in European Wages and Prices from the Middle Ages to the First World War* (Academic Press, 2001).

120 Fulbrook, 51.

121 Ibid., 65–66.

122 Ibid., 74.

123 Lynn Harry Nelson, "Lectures in Medieval History," Lawrence, Kansas, https://bit.ly/3smdsm2.

124 Here is the explanation of the calendar change that took place in 1582. Since the time of Julius Caesar, the Western world had followed Caesar's method of measuring years. He decreed that certain months would always have thirty days and others would always have thirty-one days. Then, to adjust for the fact that the March equinox reveals that the earth revolves around the sun in slightly more than 365 days, Julius Caesar stipulated that every fourth year the month of February would be increased from twenty-eight days to twenty-nine days, and this would be called a "leap year." Ever since ancient times, astronomers were aware that this method of calculating was not strictly accurate, but no one challenged the system. It was the Julian calendar, and it seemed close enough.

In 1582, Pope Gregory XIII decided something had to be done. The system that had been used for sixteen hundred years was now quite inaccurate, and this was creating a problem for the dating of Easter. Since ancient times, the church had mandated that Easter would be celebrated on the first Sunday after the first full moon that occurred either on or after the March equinox.

The actual length between March equinoxes is 365.2425 (not 365.25 as the Julian calendar assumed). So, Pope Gregory XIII mandated two changes in the system. Although every fourth year could continue to be a leap year, every calendar year divisible by one hundred (in other words, 1400, 1500, etc.) would not be a leap year, but those years divisible by four hundred (such as 1600 and 2000) would be a leap year. This makes the calendar accurately reflect solar years, which are 365.2425 days in length.

By 1582 the current calendar had drifted behind schedule, so he also mandated that the Roman Catholic world should make a one-time adjustment and skip ten days in October of 1582. That is, October 4 would be followed by October 15.

Of course, not everyone changed their calendar. The pope didn't have the authority to make countries like England, Germany or Greece change its calendar, so these countries carried on with two calendars which were noted as either "O.S." to indicate they followed the "old style" Julian calendar or "N.S." meaning they have adopted the "new style" of the Gregorian reform.

As one might expect, the solidly Roman Catholic countries such as Italy, Spain and France immediately adopted the Gregorian N.S. calendar. Prussia adopted the Gregorian calendar in 1610. Most of the other German territories waited until 1700. Great Britain waited until 1752, and Greece didn't change until 1923.

125   Johan Norberg, *Progress: The Reasons to Look Forward to the Future* (London: Oneworld Publications, 2016), 200.
126   Taylor, 79.
127   Ibid., 80.
128   Ibid., 93.
129   Ibid., 118.
130   Ibid., 121.
131   Ibid., 125.
132   Sheehan, 122.
133   "First German railroads," Wikipedia, https://bit.ly/3w7VmoA.
134   Sheehan, 342.
135   "History of Germany," Wikipedia, https://bit.ly/3M0knJi.
136   Sheehan, 342.
137   https://bit.ly/3q4EU9D.
138   Braudel, vol. 1, 311.
139   Jack Larkin, *The Reshaping of Everyday Life: 1790–1840* (New York: Harper & Row, 1988), 142.
140   Braudel, vol. 1, 299.
141   Larkin, 51.
142   Freese, 41.
143   Ibid., 32.
144   Ibid., 144.
145   Derry and Williams, 110.
146   Blum, 180.
147   Larkin, 142.
148   Ibid., 106.
149   Blum, 179.

150   Ibid.

151   Braudel, vol. 1, 275.

152   Blum, 181.

153   Sara Paston-Williams, *The Art of Dining: A History of Cooking & Eating* (The National Trust, 1993), 262.

154   Sheehan, 467.

155   Blum, 78–79.

156   Ibid., 261.

157   Sheehan, 750.

158   Blum, 95f.

159   Sheehan, 470.

160   Braudel, 531.

161   Blum, 171.

162   Ibid., 172.

163   Ibid., 118.

164   Ibid., 151.

165   Ibid., 148.

166   Ibid., 279.

167   Derry and Williams, 66.

168   Standage, 119.

169   "Legend of the Potato King," *New York Times.*

170   Blum, 274.

171   Ibid., 275.

172   Braudel, 224.

173   Blum, 296–297.

174   Ibid., 259.

175   Bernstein, 247.

176   Ibid., 248.

177   Standage, 146.

178   Braudel, 251–252.

179   Bernstein, 248–250.

180   Ibid., 247.

181   "Fork," Wikipedia, https://en.wikipedia.org/wiki/Fork.

182   Braudel, 371.

183   Standage, 133.

184   Bernstein, 133.

185   Ibid., 262.

186   Molly Harrison and O. M. Royston, *How They Lived: 1485–1700* (Ox-

ford: Basil Blackwell & Mott, Ltd., 1963), 191.
187 Ibid., 35.
188 Bernstein, 309.
189 Derry and Williams, 104.
190 Braudel, 327.
191 Derry and Williams, 104.
192 Braudel, 329.
193 "Ready-made garment," Wikipedia, https://bit.ly/3m2qul2.
194 "Trousers," Wikipedia, https://bit.ly/3N4TrbW.
195 Derry and Williams, 111.
196 Braudel, 332.
197 Larkin, 161.
198 https://thevictorianist.blogspot.com/
199 Larkin, 163f.
200 Ibid.
201 Braudel, 27.
202 Ibid., 424.
203 Scheer, 14.
204 Sheehan, 465.
205 Ibid.
206 Braudel, 430.
207 Ibid., 423.
208 "Stagecoach," Wikipedia, https://en.wikipedia.org/wiki/Stagecoach.
209 Derry and Williams, 212.
210 Braudel, 418.
211 Ibid., 369.
212 Ibid., 362.
213 Ibid., 425–428.
214 "History of rail transport in Germany," Wikipedia, https://bit.ly/38Ie-HVX.
215 Sheehan, 466.
216 Ibid.
217 Ibid., 76–80.
218 Ibid., 81.
219 Ibid., 83.
220 Ibid., 84.
221 Ibid., 88–89.
222 Ibid., 457.

223   Ibid., 83.

224   Imhof, 3f.

225   Porter, 37.

226   Ibid., 106.

227   Ibid., 39.

228   Ibid., 43.

229   Ibid., 41.

230   Ibid., 108.

231   Ibid., 48.

232   Conner, 100.

233   Ibid., 327f.

234   *Picture History of the World* (New York, NY: Grosset & Dunlap, 1979), 155.

235   Porter, 123.

236   Ibid., 124.

237   Ibid.

238   Ibid., 40.

239   Ibid., 46.

240   Conner, 407.

241   "Ignaz Semmelweis," Wikipedia, https://bit.ly/3x4FO5x.

242   Porter, 171.

243   Ibid., 93.

244   Ibid., 103.

245   Ibid., 173.

246   Ibid., 174.

247   Ibid., 114.

248   Ibid., 132f.

249   Ibid., 133.

250   Imhof, 83.

251   Standage, 126.

252   James Riley, "Estimates of Regional and Global Life Expectancy, 1800–2001," *Population and Development Review*, vol. 31, no. 3, 537–543.

253   Manchester, 55.

254   Conner, 313.

255   Porter, 140.

256   Ibid., 144.

257   Ibid., 134.

258   Ibid., 135.

259 Ibid., 136.

260 Ibid., 152.

261 Fulbrook, 72–73.

262 Blum, 69–70.

263 Imhof, 23.

264 *Picture History of the World*, 149.

265 Braudel, 393.

266 *Picture History of the World,* 149.

267 Sheehan, 227.

268 Ibid., 228.

269 Ibid., 238.

270 Blum, 147.

271 Freese, 31.

272 Sheehan, 762.

273 Blum, 29–48.

274 Ray Stannard Baker, *Seen in Germany* (London: Harper & Brothers, 1902), 17.

275 Fulbrook, 24.

276 Imhof, 60.

277 Scheer, 25.

278 Blum, 41–42.

279 Scheer, 27–30.

280 Ibid., 31–32.

281 Ibid., 35–36.

282 Ibid., 32.

283 Ibid., 16–17.

284 Ibid., 17–18.

285 Muchembled, 199.

286 Sheehan, 796.

287 Ibid., 207.

288 Ibid., 212.

289 Blum, 190.

290 Fulbrook, 90.

291 Ibid., 99.

292 Ibid., 85.

293 Sheehan, 145.

294 Ibid., 153–154.

295 Ibid., 137.

296   Ibid., 162.

297   Ibid., 146–147.

298   Larkin, 166.

299   Sheehan, 147.

300   Burkhard Sanner, "Baden-Baden: A Famous Thermal Spa with a Long History," *GHC Bulletin*, September 2000, https://bit.ly/3N2b8ry.

301   Larkin, 250.

302   Sheehan, 797.

303   Ibid., 533.

304   Ibid., 464.

305   Robert I. Weiner, *The Long 19th Century*, a thirty-six-lecture series published by The Teaching Company, Chantilly, VA, 2005, Lecture 2.

306   Weiner, Lecture 6.

307   Blum, 105.

308   Ibid., 172.

309   Ibid., 106.

310   Ibid., 97.

311   Ibid., 79.

312   Ibid., 167.

313   Ibid., 170.

314   Fulbrook, 114.

315   Ibid., 107.

316   Ibid., 122.

317   Sheehan, 72.

318   Scheer, 155–159.

319   https://bit.ly/3BQaryo.

Index

About the Author

David Koehler was born into a German American community in Des Plaines, Illinois, where his great-grandfather established the town's first hotel. David graduated from the University of Illinois with a BA in Philosophy and History, and from Yale with a BD. Now retired from the corporate world, he turns his hand to writing history. The companion to this book *Bakers, Brewers and Bricklayers: The History of Everyday German Peasants Vol. 1, 100 BCE-1450* was a finalist for the Midwest Book Award. He lives in Minneapolis with his wife of over fifty years.

www.ingramcontent.com/pod-product-compliance
Lightning Source LLC
Chambersburg PA
CBHW031950080426
42735CB00007B/333